THE WHITECHAPEL MURDERS OF 1888:
A Retrospective View

by David Holding

Published by
Words are Life, 2021

David Holding

First published in Great Britain in 2021 by
Words are Life / Scott Martin Productions
10 Chester Place,
Adlington, Chorley, PR6 9RP
wordsarelife@mail.com
www.wordsarelife.co.uk

Electronic version and paperback versions available for purchase on Amazon.
Copyright (c) David Holding and Words are Life / Scott Martin Productions.

First edition 2021.

David Holding's right to be identified as the author of this work has been asserted by him in accordance with the Copyright, Design and Patents Act 1988.

All rights reserved. Without limiting the rights under copyright reserved above, no part of this publication may be reproduced, stored or introduced into a retrieval system, or transmitted, in any form or by any means (electronic, mechanical, photocopying, recording or otherwise), without the prior written permission of both the copyright owner and the publisher of this book. No paragraph of this publication may be reproduced, copied or transmitted save with written permission or in accordance with the provisions of the Copyright Act 1956 (as amended).

Acknowledgements

It is always difficult to remember when undertaking significant research all the people who have assisted along the way with their suggestions, advice and encouragement. I wish to express my appreciation to the many academics I have consulted, ranging from such diverse disciplines as forensic science, psychology, medicine, social history and pathology, based in several universities with which I have been associated. My gratitude also extends to members of the medical and legal professions for their valuable input on the many issues raised in this work. I also wish to place on record my thanks to the largely anonymous but ever obliging staff of the institutions, libraries and archives I have contacted. My gratitude loses no sincerity in its generality. Finally, my sincere thanks must go to my publisher, Lesley Atherton. Her total commitment, professionalism and support for my work never fails to impress me.

David Holding, 2021

Dr David Holding studied history at Manchester University before entering the teaching profession in the 1970s. He taught in both state and independent sectors. It was during this time that he continued historical research culminating in the award of both a Master's degree and Doctorate.

Having previously studied law, David gained a Master of Laws degree in Medical Law, which enabled him to transfer to teaching legal courses at university. Since retiring, David has concentrated his research and writing on various aspects of local history, legal trials, forensic science and medico-legal topics.

Also By David Holding

Murder in the Heather: The Winter Hill Murder of 1838
This book is a unique account of a brutal murder which occurred on the summit of Winter Hill in Lancashire in 1838. The account draws on both contemporary media reports and court transcripts and examines the events leading up to the killing of a 21-year-old packman. It details the proceedings of the trial of the only suspect in the case. The work concludes with a re-assessment of the case in the light of modern forensic investigation. The reader is invited to reach their own 'verdict' based on the evidence provided.

The Pendle Witch Trials of 1612
The book provides readers with a sequential overview of the famous chain of events which ultimately led to the execution of women accused of practising witchcraft in the county of Lancashire. It is presented as a chronological account of the famous trials at Lancaster Castle in 1612. The reader is introduced to all the evidence and interview transcripts that formed the major plank of the prosecution case in this book that will appeal to both the general reader and local historian.

The Dark Figure: Crime in Victorian Bolton
This book provides an absorbing overview of crime in the Lancashire town of Bolton over the period 1850 to 1890. It is primarily based on documentary survey and analysis of court and police records covering the period. It assesses changes in crime over time and asks whether

these relate to economic, social or political changes taking place at the same time. The reader is left to reflect on whether crime (in all its many forms) has actually changed over time.

Bleak Christmas: The Pretoria Colliery Disaster of 1910

This work charts the events of the Lancashire Pretoria Pit disaster in December 1910. It reflects on the devastation it left within the local communities whose main source of employment was coal. The main sources analysed are the Home Office Report into the disaster and the Report of the Inquest. The findings of these detailed legal reports are presented in a format that will supplement existing material on the event. The book will also provide a reference source for both local historians and the general reader.

Doctors in the Dock: The Trials of Doctors Harold Shipman, John Bodkin Adams and Buck Ruxton

This book takes the reader on a journey into the world of three medical doctors in England, each coming from a different social background but with one common thread going through their lives. They all stood trial for murder. In each of the cases, the reader is involved from the start and is presented with all relevant evidence available to jurors in the case. The overall aim of this work is to invite readers to exercise their judgment in reaching a verdict.

Forensic Science Basics: Every Contact Leaves a Trace

Starting from the basic principles of forensic science, this work is an absorbing introductory study of the techniques familiar to us all from numerous trials, media reports and TV crime dramas. The book examines such aspects as the time of death, causes of death, weapons of crime and identification of offenders and much more. It provides essential reading for those who wish to gain a basic introduction to this fascinating area of science.

A Warning from History: The Influenza Pandemic of 1918

The 1918 Influenza Pandemic was one of the most deadly events in human history, and understanding the events and experience of 1918 is of great importance to pandemic preparation. This book aims to address questions concerning pandemic origin, features and causes, and provide the reader with an appreciation of the 1918 pandemic and its implications for future pandemics. This work will cater to both the science-orientated and general reader in this crucial area of global and public health.

The Lady Chatterley Trial Revisited
The 1960 obscenity trial of Lady Chatterley's Lover remains a symbol of freedom of expression. It is also a seminal case in British literary and social history and credited as the catalyst which encouraged frank discussion of sexual behaviour. This book introduces readers to the trial itself, describing the prosecution and defence opening and closing speeches to the jury, and much more, before culminating in the judge's summing-up of the case, and the final verdict. The reader is provided with all the evidence to reach a considered assessment of the case and a question to consider – Can certain literature 'actually' corrupt, or does it simply encourage expensive court trials and boost sales?

The Oscar Wilde Trials Revisited
It is only given to very few people to be the principal figure in three Old Bailey trials, before three different judges, and at three consecutive court sessions, all in one year. This is one of the fascinations of the Oscar Wilde trials of 1895. In addition, they embodied celebrity, sex, humorous dialogue, outstanding displays of advocacy, political intrigue, together with issues of art and morality. All these combined to ensure that trials remain memorable. Wilde's prosecution of the Marquess of Queensberry from criminal libel, and later, his own prosecution for 'gross indecency', reveal a complex person at odds with a class-centred and morally ambiguous Victorian society. This work considers these famous trials in chronological sequence and invites the reader to participate as both observer and potential juror in the proceedings. Finally, the reader is encouraged to consider the evidence presented at each of the trials, to arrive at their own conclusions. This work will be of particular interest to law students in regard to the advocacy skills so skilfully demonstrated by the respective counsel. It also caters for the general reader with a particular interest in the presentation of criminal cases in the courts in England.

Contents

Acknowledgements 3
Also By David Holding 5
Contents 7
Introduction 9
Chapter One: The Killing Ground 11
Chapter Two: The Police Investigation 14
    The Victims in Order of Their Killing 17
    The Police Reports on the Killings 18
    1) Mary Ann Nichols 19
    2) Annie Chapman 21
    3) Elizabeth Stride 22
    4) Catherine Eddowes 23
    5) Mary Jane Kelly 25
    The Medical Reports on the Victims 35
    A Pathological Overview of the Killings 42
    The Ripper Letters 45
    The Main Police Suspects for the Killings 49
    [1] Montague John Druitt 49
    [2] Severin Klosowski (Alias George Chapman) 51
    [3] Aaron Kosminski 51
    [4] John Pizer 52
    [5] Francis Tumblety 53
Chapter Three: Geographical And Psychological Profiles Of The Whitechapel Murders 63
    The Whitechapel Murders of 1888 68

The Timings of the Killings 71
A Comparable Case: The 'Yorkshire Ripper' 74
Jack The Ripper': Offender Profile 77
A Comparative Profile Of 'The Ripper' 84
Psychological Aspects Of The Murders 85
Chapter Four: An Overview Of The Case 90
Selected Bibliography 98

Introduction

This work is organised into four chapters each reflecting a sequence of the investigation of a case of serial murder. This allows the reader to compare the police investigation of the Whitechapel murders in 1888, with those of a similar investigation today. Obviously, forensic science was in its infancy at the time of the 'Ripper' enquiries, and due allowance must be accorded.

The reader is introduced to the Whitechapel area of East London to fully appreciate the socio-economic climate that the majority of its inhabitants had to endure during the latter decades of the nineteenth-century. It is against this backdrop of destitution and poverty that the five horrendous murders need to be considered.

The criminal investigation itself is examined in some detail to include the organisation of the Metropolitan Police at the time, medical and pathological reports on the victims together with their personal profiles, and a review of the main contemporary police suspects.

A chapter is devoted to an analysis of the geographical and psychological aspects of the case. It is here that the modern techniques of offender and psychological profiling are employed to throw new light on the killer's journey towards crime and the possible motives for the horrendous killings.

For over 133 years, these five homicides have remained unsolved. This gives rise to four fundamental questions which require answers:

    Who was the killer?
    What was the motive behind these killings?
    Why were the victims' bodies so mutilated?
    Why did the killings cease as suddenly as they began?

This work attempts to throw fresh light on these questions and hopefully provide some credible answers. The objective of this work is to approach the case from a purely factual perspective and to avoid the more speculative conspiracy theories that have tended to dominate other similar works on the subject of '*Jack the Ripper*'. The modern techniques now employed in the investigation of similar serial murders, geographical and offender profiling, will enable the reader to recognise patterns in the crime locations and personal characteristics of the killer.

Though contemporary media reports have been consulted, they have revealed lack of balance and objectivity in the views they expressed. On the whole, media coverage of the case tapped into the predominant pessimistic perception of the killings. This has resulted in exaggeration for dramatic effect of the actual crimes, obviously with the aim of boosting sales figures. It is one of the essential tasks of crime historians to divide fact from legend, whilst still retaining both. Each are valuable sources when set within the contemporary context. Unfortunately, in the case of some publications on the 'Ripper' murders, there are difficulties in distinguishing between baseless speculation and verifiable fact.

This work incorporates recently released source material, together with contemporary accounts to provide the reader with an accurate and reliable source of evidence on which to reach a balanced and informed conclusion to this fascinating unsolved case of serial murder. The reader is left with the question which the late Stephen Knight posed in his work: *Jack the Ripper: The Final Solution*, "*Is it possible after nearly 130 years of conjecture and deception, to get back to the basics of this crime?*" It is hoped that this work goes some way to providing an answer to this thought-provoking question...

Chapter One: The Killing Ground

The term 'East End' has been used to describe an area of London that runs eastward outside the boundary of the old city limits, towards the large docks north of the Thames. From the mid-nineteenth century, it became synonymous with the slang expression 'the black-spot'.

Charles Booth, in his famous work of 1902, *Life and Labour of the London Poor*, described it as a place of "misery, vice, and a cesspool into which the most degraded had sunk".

Falling within the Borough of Stepney were the districts of Whitechapel, Spitalfields, Shoreditch, Shadwell, Wapping, Limehouse and St George's-in-the-East.

In the late Victorian period, Whitechapel was considered to be the most notorious criminal area of London. In particular, the area around Flower and Dean Street was described as 'perhaps the foulest and most dangerous street in the whole of the Metropolis'.

Even the Metropolitan Police's Assistant Commissioner, Robert Anderson, at the time of the murders in 1888 recommended Whitechapel to those who take an interest in the 'dangerous classes', as one of London's 'show-places'. Robbery, violence and alcohol dependency were commonplace in the area.

In addition to its 'criminal' reputation, Whitechapel was characterised by extreme poverty, sub-standard housing, poor sanitation, homelessness and endemic prostitution. There were 233 common lodging-houses within the district, with around 8,000 people residing there on a nightly basis. The main thoroughfares running through Whitechapel were Whitechapel Road, Commercial Road, and Commercial Street, which on the surface were not particularly squalid.

However, it was the numerous warrens of courts and dark streets, running off these main routes that displayed the greatest examples of poverty and deprivation. It was from the mid- nineteenth century that Whitechapel became swollen with the influx of immigrants, particularly the Irish and Jews. The endemic poverty drove many women into prostitution. To some, it was a temporary measure during times of hardship, and to others it was a regular form of 'making ends meet'. In 1888, the Metropolitan Police estimated that there were around 1,200 prostitutes living within Whitechapel alone, with at least 62 known brothels.

Despite the apparent rampant crime in the Whitechapel area in the 1880s, the *Annual Report of the Sanitary Conditions of Whitechapel* recorded no murders in the area for the years 1886-87. This report also lists only 71 crimes involving 'violent deaths' during 1887. These figures suggest that while the Whitechapel area was 'crime ridden', murder was relatively rare.

It was estimated that in the late 1880s, around 15,000 of Whitechapel's population were homeless and unemployed. Some local men did manage to find employment on the docks and in the many shops and factories in the area. Working and housing conditions worsened, resulting in a significant economic 'underclass' developing in the area.

In the East End of London, approximately 55% of children died before reaching the age of 5 years. A double-dip recession occurred in 1876-1884 and another in 1893-1895. These caused severe unemployment and also caused wage levels to plummet, which in turn cheapened piece-labour and reduced wages to below subsistence levels.

During this time, the 'East End' of London was not a place from which it was possible to work one's way out. The area was literally one huge 'poverty trap' and

Whitechapel was endemic with economic deprivation. The dirty slum dwellings were criss-crossed by a network of alleyways, courtyards and lodging-houses, many of which fronted as brothels. The presence of large workhouses also symbolised inescapable destitution.

Historians of prostitution have tended to concentrate their observations of the second half of the nineteenth century. This is not altogether surprising, since the work of William Acton, the campaigns of Josephine Butler and the Ladies National Association, together with the impact of the *Contagious Diseases Acts* (1864, 1866 and 1869) all belong to this period.

Prostitution as such was not a criminal offence. The prostitution offences were specifically: soliciting, living off immoral earnings, and running 'houses of ill repute' or brothels. As a result, the police were not always compliant in the 'crusade' against prostitutes. Even when the horrors of the 'Ripper' murders had turned the nation's attention to the problem of prostitution, the police continued to be accused of tolerating it.

In fact, the Metropolitan Police favoured a policy of 'containment' in an area they could keep well policed. Interestingly, this policy was also adopted by police in many cities and towns throughout the country.

It is against this social and economic backdrop that the Whitechapel murders of 1888 need to be considered. Between 31st August and 9th November 1888, a period which has been appropriately described as an *'autumn of terror'*, some person or persons unknown, murdered and mutilated five prostitutes in the area of Whitechapel. It is to the police investigation of these killings that we turn in Chapter Two.

Chapter Two: The Police Investigation

The *Jack the Ripper* serial killings were primarily investigated by the Metropolitan Police Criminal Investigation Department from Scotland Yard, since four of the murders occurred within the Metropolitan Police areas. However, the City of London Police were also involved since one of the victims was killed within the boundary of the City force. It does appear, despite some comments to the contrary, that both forces were able to perform their respective duties amicably, and that they shared information.

The City of London force was responsible for policing the one-square mile covering the old city of London with its familiar institutions. The Commissioner was accountable to the Mayor and Corporation of London, then as today.

The Metropolitan Police, with its headquarters at Scotland Yard, covered all the other Boroughs surrounding the city, the Commissioner being accountable directly to the Home Secretary, again as today.

It is estimated that in 1885, there were approximately 13,319 police officers in the Metropolitan force, policing around 5 million inhabitants. The force was divided into 20 Divisions, each given a letter of the alphabet, followed by a number, as they are today.

In 1878, the Criminal Investigation Department was established at Scotland Yard, with a force of approximately 294 detectives. By the standards of the day, police officers were decently paid, with a secure position with promotion prospects, and a pension after 30 years' service.

Each constable was assigned a foot-patrol or 'beat' around a defined area. They were issued with a truncheon, handcuffs, a whistle, lamp and note-book.

In 1888, the Metropolitan Police was understaffed. Whereas the population of London was approximately 5,490,576, the police numbered only 14,261.
This number was broken down as under:

Superintendents	30
Inspectors	837
Sergeants	1,369
Constables	12,025

The structure of the Whitechapel Division (H) was, in order of seniority:

Superintendent	1
Chief Inspector	1
Inspectors	27
Sergeants	37
Constables	500

This Division was responsible for policing approximately 176,000 inhabitants in 1888. The police-to-population ratio in Whitechapel was approximately 1:300. The Metropolitan Police Commissioner was Sir Charles Warren, and the Head of the CID was Robert Anderson.

The CID based at Scotland Yard was divided into Districts, each with 60 Detective patrols, commanded by 15 Detective Inspectors and 159 Detective Sergeants.

From 1869 onwards, the Metropolitan Police Divisions were grouped into Districts, headed by a District Superintendent. These Districts were:

District	Divisions
1	G, H. J. K N & Thames Division
2	D, E, F. S, &Y.
3	A, B, C, T, & V.
4	L, M, P, R, & W.

The officer in overall charge at the Central CID Office at Scotland Yard was Superintendent John Shore. Under him were 5 Chief Inspectors, Swanson, Greenham, Neame, Butcher and Littlechild. Regarding the Whitechapel murders, three inspectors were assigned to the investigation. They were, Inspector First Class: Frederick George Abberline, and Inspectors Henry Moore and Walter Andrews.

In overall supervision of the 'Ripper' investigation at Scotland Yard was Chief Inspector Donald Sutherland. The head of Whitechapel H Division was Superintendent Thomas Arnold. There were four Detective Sergeants assigned to the Division. They were Thicke, Godley, McCarthy and Pierce.

During the course of the 'Ripper' investigation, Inspector Abberline was promoted to Central Office at Scotland Yard, and was succeeded by Detective Inspector Edmund Reid.

The Victims in Order of Their Killing

1) MARY ANN NICHOLS, also known as 'Polly Nichols'. Born Whitechapel 26 August, 1845. Killed Friday 31 August 1888. Buck's Row, Whitechapel. Throat Cut. Aged 43. Married – five children.

2) ANNIE CHAPMAN, also known as 'Dark Annie'. Born Paddington, London, 1841. Killed Saturday 8 September, 1888. Backyard of 29, Hanbury Street, Spitalfields. Throat Cut. Aged 47, Married – three children.

3) ELIZABETH STRIDE, also known as 'Long Liz'. Born Gothenburg, Sweden, 27 November, 1843. Killed Sunday 30 September, 1888. Passageway leading to Dutfield's Yard, between Numbers 40 and 42 Berner Street, Whitechapel. Throat Cut. Aged 45. Married.

4) CATHERINE EDDOWES, also known as 'Kate Conway'. Born Wolverhampton, 14 April, 1842. Killed early hours of Sunday 30 September, 1888, Mitre Square, City of London, Throat Cut. Aged 46. Co-habited. Three children.

5) MARY JANE KELLY, also known as 'Black Mary'. Born Limerick, Ireland, 1863. Killed Friday 9 November 1888, in her room at 13, Miller's Court, Dorset Street, Spitalfields. Throat Cut. Aged 25, Married.

The Police Reports on the Killings

The only documentary records likely to be free from ambiguity and exaggeration are those notes and reports made by the police officers contemporaneously at the crime scenes. These documents provide the most accurate and valuable written accounts of the Whitechapel murders of 1888.

These records were originally stored at both Scotland Yard and the Home Office. Later, in the 1970s they were transferred to the National Archives at Kew and the London Metropolitan Archives, where they are now available for public consultation. What follows are the author's interpretation and summaries of a selection of these reports.

The main source for these summaries is to be found in the following work:

SP Evans and K Skinner: *"The Ultimate Jack the Ripper Sourcebook: An Illustrated Encyclopedia"* (London, Robinson, 2000).

The above work contains the entire contents of the original *Scotland Yard Ripper Files* [Ref: MEPO 3/140 - 142] and the *Home Office Files* [Ref: A 49301 – 144/220 – A – K].

1) Mary Ann Nichols

At approximately 3:45 am on Friday 31st August, 1888, police discovered the body of a woman lying on her back with her throat cut. This was in a back yard at Buck's Row, Whitechapel. Dr Ralph Llewellyn of 152 Whitechapel Road attended the scene soon afterwards. He pronounced life extinct, stating that death had occurred only a short time before it was discovered. He directed that the body should be removed to the local mortuary for further examination.

Police Inspector J Spratling of J Division (Bethnal Green) arrived at the scene. He found that she had been disembowelled. Dr Llewellyn stated that her throat had been cut from left to right, with two more distinct cuts on the left side. The windpipe, gullet and spinal cord had been completely separated. There was a bruise believed to have been caused by a thumb, on the right lower jaw, and another on the left cheek. The abdomen had been cut open, and two small stab wounds inflicted on the private parts. These appeared to have been caused by a strong bladed knife by someone left-handed.

The Inspector made notes of the general description of the victim. She was about 45 years of age and approximately 5ft 3" tall, with a dark complexion. Her hair was dark brown and her eyes brown. She had a bruise on her left lower right jaw and left cheek. One tooth was missing from the front of her upper jaw, and two on the left of her lower jaw. The Inspector made enquiries with local residents, but none of them had heard any screams during the night. A search of the surrounding buildings and premises of the local railway company was conducted, but no weapon was discovered. A police sergeant and constable informed the Inspector that they had passed through Buck's Row at 3:15am, but there was no body there at that time. A more detailed account of the killing was written by Detective Frederick Abberline, who had been drafted in from Scotland Yard to oversee the investigation. He reported that at approximately 3:40am a car-man on his way to work passed through Buck's Row and had noticed a woman lying on her back against some gates leading into a stable yard. He stopped to look at the woman and was joined by another car-man, also on his way to work. Being still dark at the time, they did not notice any blood. These two men, on arriving at the corner of Hanbury Street and Old Montagu Street, informed a constable on duty there of what they had seen.

The constable made his way to the scene and found two other constables already there. Dr Llewellyn was summoned to the scene, and the body was removed to the mortuary. According to the doctor, the stab wounds to the abdomen were sufficient to have caused instant death. He also expressed the opinion that the stabs were inflicted before the throat was cut. At this stage, the body had not been formally identified.

On examining the victim's clothing at the mortuary, it was found that some underclothing bore the mark of Lambeth Workhouse. This enabled the body to be identified as that of former inmate, Mary Ann Nichols. In May 1888, she had left the Workhouse and found employment in Wandsworth, which lasted until early July. Shortly afterwards she became a lodger at 18, Thrawl Street, Spitalfields. At approximately 1:40am on the morning of Friday 31st August, she was seen in the kitchen of her lodgings by the deputy of the lodging-house, who she informed that she had no money to pay for her lodgings. She left the buildings telling him that she would return with some money. At the time, she appeared to be worse for drink.

She was next seen at 2:30am by Ellen Holland, a fellow lodger, at the corner of Osborn Street and

Whitechapel Road. This witness stated that Mary was very drunk and that she had persuaded her to return with her to the lodgings. Mary had refused and walked away down Whitechapel Road in the general direction of Buck's Row. This witness was in no doubt about the time when she saw Mary, because the Whitechapel church clock struck 2:30am. The distance from Osborn Street to Buck's Row would be about half a mile.

2) Annie Chapman

At approximately 6:10am on Saturday 8th September, 1888, Inspector Joseph Chandler was on duty at Commercial Street Police Station, Spitalfields, when he received information that a woman had been discovered in Hanbury Street. He made his way to the scene arriving at 29, Hanbury Street, and found a woman lying on her back in the back yard of the premises. Her left arm was lying across her left breast, and her small intestine was lying above her right shoulder. Her throat had been cut deeply from the left around her throat in a jagged manner.

Inspector Chandler summoned Dr George Phillips, the Divisional police surgeon to attend the scene, and also sent for the ambulance and police assistance. On his arrival at the scene, Dr Phillips pronounced life extinct and remarked that the woman had been dead for at least two hours prior to her discovery. The body was then removed by police ambulance to Whitechapel Mortuary.

The Inspector had examined the backyard of the premises and found on the back wall about 18 inches above the ground six patches of blood, together with smaller patches on the wooden fencing.

The woman was identified by the deputy of Crossingham's lodging-house, Timothy Donovan of 35, Dorset Street, Spitalfields, as one of his lodgers named Annie Chapman. He had known her for about 16 months as a prostitute in the area. She had lodged at his property for about four months. Donovan stated that he had seen her in the kitchen of the property at 1:45am on the morning of Saturday 8th September, and she was drunk. Inspector Chandler provided a description of the deceased. She was approximately 45 years of age and about 5ft tall, with fair complexion, dark brown hair and blue eyes. She had two teeth missing from her lower jaw. This description was circulated by telegraph to all police stations.

A special enquiry was made at lodging-houses for any lodgers with blood on their clothing and who had entered the premises after 2:00am that morning. The victim had been a frequent lodger in the neighbourhood of Spitalfields before residing at 35, Dorset Street. She was last seen alive at 2:00am.

On the morning of the murder, several witnesses were interviewed regarding the movements of the victim. A John Richardson, also of 29, Hanbury Street, was outside in the back yard at 4:45am, but saw no body there at that time. Another neighbour, Albert Cadosch of 27, Hanbury Street, was in the back yard at 5:25am and heard someone talking in the yard of number 29, and then heard a noise like something falling against the communal fencing between number 27 and 29.

3) Elizabeth Stride

The only report on this murder is to the Home Office and was compiled by Detective Chief Inspector Donald Swanson from Scotland Yard, dated 19 October, 1888. At approximately 1:00am on the morning of Sunday 30 September, 1888, the body of a woman was found with the throat cut but otherwise not mutilated, inside the gates of Dutfield's Yard, in Berner Street, off Commercial Road East, Whitechapel. The body was discovered by Louis Diemschutz, Secretary of the Socialist Club. This information was passed to the police who sent for Doctors Blackwell and Phillips. At 1:10am, the body was examined by both doctors and life was pronounced extinct. The body was lying on the left side, with the left arm extended from the elbow. The right hand was over the stomach. The back of the hand and inner surface of the wrist were dotted with blood. The body was still warm to the touch. There was a silk handkerchief around the throat, which was deeply gashed. A search was made in the yard, but no instrument found.

The body was that of Elizabeth Stride, a prostitute. All members of the Socialist Club who were present, were searched and their clothes were examined, then statements taken. Enquiries were made in Berner Street if any person was seen with the woman at the time. Leaflets were printed and distributed in H Division, requesting that occupiers provide information of any suspicious persons lodging in their homes. The statements taken were checked and the persons required to account for their movements at the time of the murder.

House-to-house enquiries were conducted, lodging houses visited, and over 2,000 lodgers questioned. Enquiries were also made by Thames Police regarding sailors on board ships in the docks and on the river. Seventy-six butchers and slaughtermen were visited, and checks were made on those employed in these trades.

4) Catherine Eddowes

A report of the murder was compiled by Detective Chief Inspector Donald Swanson, dated 6 November, 1888. On Sunday, 30th September, 1888 at approximately 1:45am, a City of London police constable discovered the body of a woman in Mitre Square. Her face had been mutilated beyond recognition. A portion of her nose had been cut off, and the lobe of the right ear was nearly severed. The throat had been cut and the body disembowelled.

At approximately 1:30am, the same police constable had passed the spot where the body was found, and there was nothing to be seen. At about 1:35am, three Jewish gentlemen saw a man talking to a woman in Church Passage, which led directly into Mitre Square. They could not provide a description of this man.

At 2:20am, another constable from the City Police stated that he visited Goulston Street Dwellings on his beat, and there was nothing there at that time. However, on revisiting the same area at 2:55am, he found a piece of a bloodstained apron at the bottom of the stairway leading up to numbers 108-119. Above it, the following was written in chalk on the wall:

"The Jewes are the men who will not be blamed for nothing".

It was established that the piece of apron found by the constable corresponded exactly with the part missing from the body of the mutilated body. Two doctors attended the scene, Dr Frederick Brown, the City Police surgeon, and Dr Phillips, called by the Metropolitan Police who were attending the scene.

The result of the post-mortem revealed that the left kidney was missing from the body, together with the uterus. It was the doctors' opinion that the mutilations provided no evidence of anatomical knowledge. However, it was also expressed that the murder could have been carried out by such persons as butchers or slaughtermen, as well as by medical students.

The City Police enquiries revealed that beside the body were found some pawn tickets in a tin box which related to pledges made by the deceased. The victim's name was Catherine Eddowes and she had been arrested for drunkenness at Bishopsgate Street Police Station at 8:45pm on Saturday 29 September, and then discharged when sober at 1:00am on the 30 September.

Upon discovery of the chalk writing on the wall at Goulston Dwellings (which were occupied exclusively by Jews), the Metropolitan Police Commissioner ordered that the writing should be rubbed out. He believed that the writing was intended to throw the blame upon the Jews, and he wanted to avoid the possibility of disorder arising.

It appears that enquiries of the City of London Police had merged into those of the Metropolitan Police at this stage.

5) Mary Jane Kelly

The final murder occurred on Friday 9 November, 1888, and it took place in the victim's own room at 13, Miller's Court, Dorset Street, Spitalfields. However, an official record of events surrounding the murder doesn't exist.

The Middlesex County Records Office houses a collection of original statements of witnesses interviewed on the morning of the death of Mary Kelly. Of particular interest is that they are in the handwriting of Detective Inspector Frederick Abberline.

[1] Statement of Thomas Bowyer, 37, Dorset Street, Spitalfields, employed by John McCarthy, Lodging-house keeper, Dorset Street.

At 10:45am on the 9 November, he was sent by his employer to Room 13, at Miller's Court for the rent. He could not gain entry, and on looking through the window, he saw the body of Mary Jane Kelly. Discovering blood on her body, he immediately informed Mr McCarthy of what he had seen. He sent Boyer to the police station in Commercial Street, and he informed the duty inspector there, who returned with him to the scene.

[2] Statement of John McCarthy, Lodging-house Keeper, 27, Dorset Street, Spitalfields

He sent Thomas Bowyer to Room 13 Miller's Court, Dorset Street, owned by him, for the rent. "He reported what he had seen, and I went back with him. Looking through the window, I saw the mutilated body of the deceased. I knew her as Mary Jane Kelly. I sent Bowyer to the Police Station and followed there myself. The Inspector returned with both of us."

[3] Statement of Joseph Barnett of 24, New Street, Bishopsgate.

He stated that he was a porter at Billingsgate Market but had been unemployed for four months. He had been living with Mary Jane Kelly at Room 13, Miller's Court for the past eight months. On Tuesday 30 October, he left her because of her resorting to prostitution, but remained friendly with her. He visited her between 7:00 and 8:00pm on Thursday 8 November, and then left, and that was the last time he saw her alive.

[4] Statement of Mary Ann Cox, Room 5, Miller's Court, Dorset Street, Spitalfields.

She stated that she was a widow and prostitute and had known the occupant of Room 13 for about eight months. She knew her as Mary Jane. About 11:45pm the previous night (8 November), she came into Dorset Street from Commercial Street and saw Mary Jane walking in front of her with a man. They turned into Miller's Court and went indoors. Mary appeared very drunk at the time, and shortly afterwards the witness heard Mary singing. The witness went out soon after 12:00 and returned at about 1:00am. Mary was still singing. She then went out again shortly after 1:00am and returned at 3:00am. There was no light in Mary's room, and all was quiet. "The man I saw her with would be about 36 years of age, about 5' 5" with a fresh complexion. He had small side-whiskers and a thick moustache, and was wearing a dark overcoat and a black hat."

[5] Statement of Elizabeth Prater, wife of William Prater of Room 20, 27 Dorset Street, Spitalfields

She stated that she went out around 9:00pm on the 8 November, returning at about 1:00am on the 9th., and stood at the bottom of Miller's Court until approximately 1:30am. She then went to bed, but was woken up by a kitten walking over her neck. At that time, she heard screams of 'murder' two or three times in a woman's voice. She did not pay too much attention to the cries because they were a common occurrence coming from the back of the lodging-house in Miller's Court. During the time between 1:00 and 1:30am, she saw no one in the court. She got downstairs and into the court at about 5:30am, and saw only two or three men with their horses in Dorset Street. She went out to the local public house, the 'Ten Bells' at the corner of Church Street, then returned back home and went to bed until 11am.

[6] Statement of Caroline Maxwell, 14, Dorset Street, Spitalfields, wife of Henry Maxwell, lodging-house deputy

She stated that she had known the deceased woman for around four months, and knew her as Mary Jane. She earned her living as a prostitute. She had not seen Mary for about three weeks until Friday 9 November, at about 8:30am. She had been standing at the corner of Miller's Court in Dorset Street. "She told me that she had been drinking for a number of days and was suffering the effects. I then left her to go to Bishopsgate on an errand. I returned to Dorset Street at about 9:00am. I noticed that Mary Jane was standing outside the Britannia public house, talking to a man." She described him as being about 30 years old, 5' 5" tall, dressed as a Market Porter. Being some distance away, she doubted whether she would be able to identify him.

Kelly being seen by Caroline Maxwell at 9:00am contradicts the medical evidence, which showed that Kelly had been dead at least 5 or 6 hours before her body was discovered at 10:45am.

[7] Statement of Sarah Lewis, Laundress, from 24, Great Pearl Street, Spitalfields

She stated that between 2 and 3am on the morning of 9 November, she had visited at Keylers at 2, Miller's Court. As she was going up the court, she saw a man standing against the lodging-house on the opposite side to Miller's Court in Dorset Street. She could not describe him. Just before 4:00am, she heard a scream of a young woman not far away from her. She did not look out of her window. She did not know Mary Jane.

[8] Statement of Julia Venturney

She stated that she occupied Room 1 at Miller's Court. She was a widow, but was living with Harry Owen. On the night of Thursday 8 November, she was awake all night as she was unable to sleep. She had known the lodger in Room 13 for about four months. She knew Joe Barnett who had lived with Mary Jane until recently. She had heard him say that he did not like Mary Jane going out on the streets. He did frequently give her money and was kind to her but said he would not continue to live with Mary Jane while she continued her immoral ways. The witness also stated that Mary Jane occasionally got drunk. She last saw her at about 10am.

[9] Statement of Maria Harvey, 3, New Court, Dorset Street

The witness stated that she had spent the Monday and Tuesday of the week (5 and 6 November) sleeping with Mary Jane Kelly. She saw Mary on Thursday 8 at about 6:55pm when Joe Barnett called on her. She then left them together.

These Statements were handwritten by Detective Inspector Frederick Abberline.

The Victim's Background

[1] Mary Ann Nichols

Born in London in 1845, she was the daughter of a locksmith Edward Walker, of Dean Street, Fetters Lane in the City. In 1864, 19-year-old Mary married William Nichols, a printer of Bouverie Street, where they lived briefly when first married. They moved to live with Mary Ann's father at 131 Trafalgar Street, Walworth. Between 1864 and 1870, Mary had three children, Edward John in 1864, Percy George in 1868 and Alice Esther in 1870. They moved again in July 1876 to a place of their own at Tenement No 3, Peabody Buildings, in Duchy Street, Stamford Estate, Lambeth. Two more children were born there, Eliza Sarah in 1876 and Henry Alfred in 1878.

By this stage, things were going bad. Mary Ann had begun drinking heavily and, on a number of occasions, she did move out of the family home but eventually returned. Her husband, William, had become friendly with another woman known to Mary Ann. Eventually, in 1880, they separated, with William keeping the children, except Edward John who went to live with Mary Ann. It is known that William paid Mary Ann a weekly allowance of five shillings (the equivalent of about £12 today). This continued until 1882 when he discovered that Mary Ann was earning money as a prostitute.

From then on, her lifestyle degenerated. From September 1880 until May 1881, she was an inmate of Lambeth Workhouse. Then, in 1883, she returned to live with her father, but as a result of her constant drinking, and a quarrel with her father, she left in May of 1884. After another spell in Lambeth Workhouse, she settled into 15, York Street, Walworth where she lived with a blacksmith named Stuart Drew. This cohabitation lasted until 1887 when she sold some of Drew's possessions to buy drink. Drew left her, and she returned to the workhouse. She made one final effort at respectability in April 1888, when she entered the service of a Mr Samuel Cowdry and his wife Sarah in Wandsworth.

However, in July of that year, Mary Ann absconded from the Cowdry's taking with her a bundle of stolen clothes valued at £3.10s. She then returned to the workhouse before finding refuge at a doss-house at Number 36, Flower and Dean Street. Mary Ann's sad life came to an end on 31 August, 1888 on the pavement in Buck's Row, Whitechapel.

[2] Annie Chapman
Born Eliza Annie Chapman in Paddington in 1841, her father George Smith, a shoemaker, enlisted in the Life Guards in December 1834 and married Ruth Chapman in 1846. Annie was 15 when the family moved to Windsor in 1856. In 1869, Annie then 28 years old, married John Chapman in Knightsbridge. They lived in West London until 1882 when they moved back to Windsor.

Annie had two daughters, Emily Ruth in 1870 and Anne Georgina in 1873 and a disabled son John Alfred in 1880. Sadly, Emily died of meningitis in 1882, and shortly before her death, Annie began to exhibit signs of restlessness. She abandoned her family and returned to London alone. It could be that her alcoholism and immorality broke up the marriage. However, up to the time of his death in 1886, her husband continued to send her occasional sums of money. When the allowance ceased, Annie managed to scrape a living selling matches or flowers. She also accepted pieces of financial help from friends. When all else failed, she resorted to prostitution.

During 1886 she was living at 30 Dorset Street with a sieve-maker, but from around May 1888, she was living at Crossingham's Lodging House at 35, Dorset Street, Whitechapel.

[3] Elizabeth Stride

Elizabeth was the daughter of Swedish farmer Gustaf Ericsson from Torslanda near Gothenburg, and was born in 1843. She moved in 1860 when she was 17 into Gothenburg itself, finding work as a domestic servant. Then, in 1864, she left the service, and by March 1865 she was registered by the police in Gothenburg as a 'professional prostitute'. Elizabeth's mother died in 1864, and, on receiving a substantial inheritance, she applied for and was granted permission to move to London, sailing on the 7 February 1866. On 7 March 1869 giving her maiden name as Gustafsson and her address as 76, Gower Street, she married John Thomas Stride, and they opened a coffee shop in Upper North Street, Poplar.

However, on 21 March 1877, she was taken by the police from Thames Magistrates' Court, Arbour Square, Stepney, to the Poplar Workhouse. In 1881, the couple were living together in Bow, but the marriage was in trouble. In December 1881, Elizabeth was being nursed following an attack of bronchitis in the Whitechapel Workhouse Infirmary. Whilst there, she gave her home address as a lodging house in Brick Lane. On leaving the Infirmary, she moved into a lodging house at 32 Flower and Dean Street, Whitechapel.

By 1885, she was living with Michael Kidney, a labourer in his early thirties at 38 Dorset Street. He was a rough and violent person, and she brought a charge of assault against him. He drank heavily, and she appears to have also been overfond of the bottle. She managed to amass eight convictions for drunkenness in the final year of her short life, which ended abruptly on 30 September 1888.

[4] Catherine Eddowes

Catherine was born in Wolverhampton on 14 April 1842. She had a brother and four sisters, the family eventually being increased by the addition of four more brothers and two sisters. The sizeable family moved to Bermondsey before Catherine was two years old. Her mother, Catherine died of TB in 1855, when Catherine was only 13. Then in 1857, her father also died.

After her mother's death, most of the children were sent to Bermondsey Workhouse and Industrial School. Catherine went on to Dowgate Charity School in the City of London. According to the 1861 census, Catherine was then living back in Wolverhampton with her aunt Elizabeth Eddowes, her husband William and their three children. Catherine worked as a tin plate stamper at an engineering works in Wolverhampton, where he uncle William also worked.

It transpired that Catherine was sacked in 1862 for stealing and ran away to Birmingham with another of her uncles, Thomas Eddowes, a shoemaker. During 1862, Catherine met a 24-year-old man, Thomas Conway, in Birmingham. He had been invalided out of the army on a military pension. Catherine gave the impression that she was legitimately married to Conway, but this was incorrect. They had three children, and by 1881 they had moved to Chelsea in London.

Later the same year, the Conways separated. Her husband took his sons with him. The separation was blamed on Catherine's drinking. She was slipping into alcoholism, witnessed by periodic absences from home. It is, however, likely that she was subjected to brutal treatment by Conway. She made her way to Spitalfields, where her widowed sister Eliza was living. When times were hard, Catherine turned to prostitution.

At other times, she earned a little money working for the Jewish community in Brick Lane, Whitechapel.

Eventually, she joined forces with an Irish labourer and market porter named John Kelly. She went to live with him in lodgings at 55, Flower and Dean Street. This partnership lasted, and she was still with him in 1888 until Sunday 30 September when the Ripper struck again.

[5] Mary Jane Kelly

Mary was born in Castletown, County Limerick in Ireland in 1864, to John Kelly and Ann McCarthy. She had two brothers: John born in 1866, and Peter born in 1868. If Kelly's landlord John McCarthy was related to her mother, possibly being Mary Jane's uncle, this may explain why he allowed her to be six weeks in arrears with her rent in London.

During her early years in London, she had been in a shelter run by nuns at the Providence Row Night Refuge in Crispin Street, opposite Dorset Street, Spitalfields. She stayed there briefly and was found employment in domestic service but disliked it and took to the streets. There was a question of whether the body discovered in Miller's Court was pregnant. However, in 1987, the post-mortem report on Mary Jane's death was received by Scotland Yard. This made it clear that Mary Kelly's womb was neither stolen nor gravid. It lay with her kidneys and one severed breast, under her head at the scene of the killing.

The Medical Reports on the Victims

[1] Mary Ann Nichols
Report by Dr Rees Ralph Llewellyn

Dr Llewellyn examined the body of the deceased at 4am on the 31 August 1888. He decided that the killing had been committed on the spot in Buck's Row where the body lay. He observed facial bruising, the possible result of a blow from a fist, or it could have been caused by the pressure of a thumb and fingers. He saw body wounds inflicted by a knife, strong-bladed, moderately sharp, being used violently in a downward direction. No part of the viscera was missing. The throat had been cut which practically severed the victim's head from her body. There were several incisions in the abdomen. He believed that the attacker was a left-handed person.

[2] Annie Chapman
Report by Dr George Phillips

Dr Phillips attended the scene at Hanbury Street at 6:10am on the 8 September 1888. He concluded that the woman's breathing had been restricted prior to her death. He found her face swollen, as was her tongue. These were both signs of suffocation. He thought that the attacker had taken hold of the woman by the chin, lowered her to the ground, and then cut her throat deeply. The muscular structure of the neck appeared as though an attempt had been made to separate the cervical vertebrae.

Death was attributed to heart failure caused by the loss of blood from the throat wound. The body had been mutilated, but Phillips was satisfied that the mutilations had been carried out *post-mortem*. The parts missing from the body were the uterus and its appendages, the upper part of the vagina, and two-thirds of the bladder. The cutting of the throat was from left to right. He thought that the instrument which caused the mutilations would not be an ordinary knife. It had to be a very sharp and thin, narrow blade at least 6 to 8 inches in length. It could have been a knife of the sort used for post-mortem dissection. The sort of knife used by slaughtermen or butchers if well ground down might produce the same kind of wounds. He concluded that the incision could have been made by one sweep of the knife. This would be indicative that the attacker possessed both anatomical knowledge and expertise.

These final comments from Dr Phillips indicated the possible direction in which a search to locate the Whitechapel murderer could be instigated.

[3] Elizabeth Stride
Report by Dr Frederick William Blackwell

Dr Blackwell attended the scene at 1:10pm at Berner Street on Sunday, 30 September, 1888. In addition, Dr George Phillips had also been summoned to attend the scene. Whilst awaiting the arrival of Dr Phillips, Dr Blackwell made the following observations:

> "There was a check silk scarf round the neck, the bow of which was turned to the left side and pulled tightly. There was a long incision in the neck, which exactly corresponded with the lower border of the scarf. The lower edge of the scarf was slightly frayed as if by a sharp knife. The blood was running down in the gutter into the drain. It was running in an opposite direction to the feet. There was a quantity of clotted blood just under the body. I formed the opinion that the murderer first took hold of the silk scarf, at the back of it, and then pulled the deceased backwards, but I cannot say whether the throat was cut while the woman was standing or after she was pulled backwards. The deceased would take about a minute and a half

to bleed to death".

On arrival at Berner Street, Dr Phillips made a preliminary examination at the scene. The following day, Dr Phillips shared the post-mortem with Dr Blackwell. The doctors' attention was drawn to the appearance over both of the shoulders, under the clavicle and also in front of the chest, of a bluish discolouration.

This led Dr Blackwell to believe that the deceased had been seized by the shoulders and forced to the ground. Then, with the assailant crouching at her right side, her throat was cut. The 6-inch incision, inflicted from left to right, practically severed the carotid artery, and the victim died as a result of the haemorrhage and the cutting of her trachea.

Regarding the weapon used, Dr Phillips did not think it would be a knife anything as long as 9 inches. Also, there was no indication of the use of a pointed knife. Chapman's neck had been mutilated in exactly the same way as Mary Jane Kelly.

Dr Phillips also observed that in the case of Stride, the murderer would not necessarily be blood-stained. The wound and the injury to the blood vessels would be such as to direct the blood stream away from him.

[4] Catherine Eddowes
Report by Dr George William Sequiera

The doctor arrived at the scene in Mitre Square at 1:55am on Monday 1 October 1888. He remained at the scene while Dr Frederick Brown, the City police surgeon arrived at approximately 2:18am.

Dr Sequiera did not think that the perpetrator had any great anatomical skill and nor was he searching for any particular organs. He accounted for the lack of any noise from the victim because death had been instantaneous after the severance of the windpipe and the blood vessels.

Judging from the condition of the blood, he had decided that life had been extinct no more than about 15 minutes. After viewing Eddowes' body *in situ,* Dr Brown ordered it to be removed to the City Mortuary for a post-mortem examination.

At Brown's request, Dr Phillips attended. Dr Brown considered that the knife-work in this case suggested a good knowledge of the positions of the organs in the abdominal cavity and the way of removing them. He suggested that the instrument employed would be sharp, pointed, knife-like and some 6 inches in length.

His view was that the victim was lying on the ground at the time of the attack. Her throat had been cut from left to right, the larynx being severed below the vocal cords. All the deep cervical structures had been cut through to the bone, knife notches marking the cartilage. The cause of death was given as haemorrhage from the left carotid artery. He also confirmed that the mutilations took place post-mortem.

Missing from the body were the uterus and the left-kidney. Not removed were the cervix of the womb and the vagina, both of which were uninjured. Dr Phillips was of the opinion that the attacker exhibited a degree of knowledge and dexterity that might be characteristic of someone accustomed to butchering animals.

No traces of any sexual activity were found on the body. Present at Eddowes' post-mortem was Dr William Sandes who was the public analyst for the City of London. He did not consider that the killer had displayed any anatomical skill, and nothing led him to believe that he had any particular organ in mind. Sandes looked for, but failed to find, any poison in the contents of Eddowes' stomach.

[5] Mary Jane Kelly
Report by Dr George Phillips
Dr Phillips was called by police at 11:00am on

Friday 9 November 1888, and at approximately 11:15am he entered Miller's Court to view the butchered body of Mary Jane Kelly. At the inquest into the death, held on 12 November, 1888, it was reported in *The Times* on the 13 November:

> "Finding the door to Number 13 Miller's Court locked, it was not until 1:30pm when the door was forced open that Dr Phillips entered the room. The mutilated remains of a female were lying two-thirds over towards the edge of a bedstead nearest the door. I am sure the body had been removed subsequently to the injury which caused death; from that side of the bedstead which was nearest to the wooden partition, because of the large quantity of blood under the bedstead, and the saturated condition of the sheet at the top corner nearest the partition. The blood was produced by the severing of the right carotid artery, which was the immediate cause of death. This injury was inflicted while the deceased was lying at the right side of the bedstead".

The post-mortem had been carried out at Shoreditch Mortuary in the presence of Dr Thomas Bond, the divisional police surgeon to A-Whitehall Division of the Metropolitan Police. When he was summoned to Miller's Court, he made his post-mortem observations in the victim's room at 2:00pm on the day of the discovery of the body - 9 November 1888. He reported as follows:

> "The viscera were found in various parts, the uterus and kidneys with one breast, under the head, the other breast by the right foot, the liver between the feet, the intestines by the right side and the spleen by the left side of the body. The stomach was attached to the intestines. The

right lining remained in the thoracic cavity, its lower part broken and torn away. The left lung was intact, the pericardium was open below, and the heart missing from the sac. The neck was cut through the skin and other tissues right down to the vertebrae".

Dr Bond also submitted to the police, a general report on the murders of Nichols, Chapman, Stride and Eddowes, based on the medical notes written by the other doctors. As regards generalisations about the killings, Bond's conclusions were that in the cases of Nichols, Chapman, Stride and Eddowes, the throats appeared to have been cut from left to right. In the case of Kelly, owing to extensive mutilation, it was impossible to say in what direction the fatal cut was made, but arterial blood was found on the wall in splashes close to where the woman's head must have been lying.

All the circumstances surrounding the murders led him to form the opinion that the women must have been lying down when murdered, and in every case, the throat was cut first. In all cases, there appeared to be no evidence of struggling, and the attacks were probably so sudden and made in such a position that the women could neither resist nor cry out.

In the first four cases, the murderer must have attacked from the right side of the victims.

In the Kelly case, he must have attacked in front as there would be no room for him between the wall and the part of the bed on which the woman was lying.

In Bond's opinion, the murderer would not necessarily have been splashed with blood, although there must have been some degree of smearing of his hands, arms and parts of his clothing.

In every case, except Elizabeth, the mutilations were the same, which made it clear that the object was mutilation.

Bond did not think the offender had any scientific or anatomical knowledge. His hazard as to the instrument used was "a strong knife at least 6 inches long and very sharp, pointed at the top and about 1 inch wide". It may have been a clasp-knife, a butcher's knife or a surgeon's knife, but it was a straight knife.

A Pathological Overview of the Killings

Professor Francis Camps, Professor of Forensic Medicine at the London Hospital Medical School, Whitechapel, takes a new look at the post-mortem evidence in the 'Ripper' killings of 1888.

His attention was drawn to the fact that the wounds and mutilations inflicted on the victims were accompanied by far less spillage of blood than might have been expected. According to the witness statements, there was very little blood on the pavement in Buck's Row, considering the extent of the wounds on Mary Ann Nichol's body.

This was noted by Inspector Joseph Chandler, who also noted that there were relatively small amounts of blood in the Hanbury Street yard where Annie Chapman was butchered, together with just a few bloodstains on the wall close to the body. Camps argued, "...this is in direct contradiction with the fact that they were all stated to have died without calling out". He then posed the question: "The police failed to identify or arrest the Ripper in 1888, would they, if he returned, do any better today?"

In 1888, fingerprint identification was not available as a practical science. Although the Ripper must have left a great many behind, the police lacked the means to exploit them. After the Eddowes murder, it appears that the murderer washed blood off his hands at a public sink set back in a close off Dorset Street. He then wiped them on a piece of an apron which he dropped in the passages leading to the staircase of number 108 to 119 Wentworth Dwellings.

Modern forensic techniques might have revealed by blood grouping, whether the blood in the water and on the fragment of the apron belonged to the victim. A blood-stained knife with a 10-inch blade was found in the Whitechapel Road near the London Hospital.

Dr George Phillips, one of the medical men, called to the scene of the Eddowes killing, doubted if it was the weapon used in the attack. Modern methods could have revealed conclusive blood or fingerprint evidence.

There was a display of carelessness in the handling of the body in the case of Mary Ann Nichols. Not even the police surgeon, Dr Llewellyn, who called at Buck's Row, noticed the extent and nature of the woman's injuries at first.

The blood was washed off the victim before any competent person could examine the scene of the murder to assess that the likelihood that the wounds had been made after death. Also, the body had been removed before a search for possible vital clues and trace evidence was undertaken. When the body did arrive at Old Montagu Street Workhouse Mortuary, it was undressed and washed before Dr Llewellyn carried out the post-mortem examination. Likewise, Annie Chapman's body was undressed and washed before its examination by Dr Phillips, one of the other police surgeons involved in the investigation.

It was only after the removal of a handkerchief that was wrapped around the neck, that Dr Phillips noticed that the head had been almost completely severed from the body. Camps, in his commentary of the investigation, is very critical of what he calls "the singular lack of co-operation between the doctors and the police in assessing evidence".

At no stage did they appear to have discussed the Chapman case. In two of the other cases, there was development by the police of theories of their own which were quite irrelevant to the doctors' findings. In this instance, he was obviously referring to the fact that the police had their own pet theory that Mary Ann Nichols had been attacked from behind, which was not the view of the doctor who attended the scene. They also insisted that the murderer of Annie Chapman must have been covered with blood, despite the medical opinion that the injuries had been inflicted 'post- mortem'.

On balance, Camps is of the opinion that, although the Ripper would have had a much more difficult task in eluding the police today, the likelihood is that he still would not have been caught.

Source: Francis Camps, *The Investigation of Murder*, (London, Michael Joseph, 1966)

During the police investigation of the killings in 1888, there was evidence of a 'policy of reticence on the part of the police, defensible on the ground that it was a precaution' to prevent villains being forewarned as to what the CID knew, and might do. This could also be viewed as a policy of positive suppression and overt antagonism towards the press.

This inevitably led reporters to 'create' news which could or could not be false. The truth is that fiercely competing journalists were often so starved of facts from official sources, that an inevitable market for gossip, hearsay and uncorroborated reports emerged. So, although there was a considerable amount of good, sound and honest newspaper coverage of the Whitechapel killings, there was also quite a large segment that was totally fiction.

When in the 1970s, police and Home Office records on the case became available to the public, many writers on the subject took advantage and consulted them. Now available are the first entirely authentic accounts of each of the generally accepted five Whitechapel 'Ripper' murders. These are now housed at the National Archives in Kew.

The Ripper Letters

The origin of the mythology of 'Jack the Ripper' lies in the communications that the killer allegedly sent to the media and the police at the time of the Whitechapel murders. Although there is no evidence to support the theory that the real killer was involved in the production of these letters, more than 200 'Jack the Ripper' letters contributed to the creation and popularisation of the name and persona of 'Jack the Ripper'. Despite the large number of letters involved in the case, it was only a small number of these letters that received serious investigative attention from the police at the time.

Probably the most significant text in the whole case is the *'Dear Boss'* letter, received on the 27 September 1888, by the Central News Agency in London. This letter is the first ever signed as *'Jack the Ripper'*. It is this letter that is responsible for the creation of the pseudonym.

This letter claimed responsibility for the murder of Annie Chapman on 8 September 1888. It mentioned that an ear would be cut off the next victim and sent to the police. Indeed, the murder of Chapman was followed by another in which part of one ear of the victim was removed, but this was never sent to the police. Because of this fact and its style and content, the letter was considered genuine. It became famous (or infamous) for introducing the persona of 'Jack the Ripper', and for providing a name that the press could use to refer to the killer. The text of this letter is reproduced below:

25 Sept. 1888

"Dear Boss,

I keep on hearing the police have caught me but they wont fix me just yet. I have laughed when they look so clever and talk about being on the right track. That joke about Leather Apron gave me real fits. I am down on whores and I shant quit ripping them till I get buckled. Grand work that last job was. I gave the lady no time to squeal. How can they catch me now. I love my work and want to start again. You will soon hear of me with my funny little games. I saved some of the proper red stuff in a ginger beer bottle but it went thick like glue, and I cant use it. Red ink is fit enough I hope, ha ha. The next job I do I shall clip the lady's ears off and send to the police officers just for jolly, wouldnt you. Keep this letter back till I do a bit more work, then give it out straight. My knife's nice and sharp. I want to get to work right away if I get a chance.
Yours truly,
Jack the Ripper.
Don't mind me giving the trade name."

Written at right angles to the rest of this letter was the following:

"Wasnt good enough to post this before I got all the red ink off my hands, curse it. No luck yet. They say, I'm a doctor now, ha ha".

This first letter was received by the Central News Agency on 27 September, then forwarded to the Metropolitan Police on 29 September. The second most important text is the '*Saucy Jacky*' postcard posted on 30 September and received on 1 October 1888 by the Central

News Agency, signed as 'Jack the Ripper'. This postcard claimed responsibility for the double murders of Elizabeth Stride and Catherine Eddowes, on the night of 30 September. The postcard did not threaten future murders, and presented an apology for not having sent an ear to the police. The text of this postcard is reproduced below:

> "I was not codding dear old Boss when I gave you the tip, youll hear about Saucy Jacky, a work tomorrow double event this time. Number one squeeled a bit so couldn't finish straight off. Had not time to get ears for police. Thanks for keeping last letter back until I got to work again. Jack the Ripper"

This postcard was the second communication received by the Central News Agency. It was posted on 30 September, the day after the 'Double Event'. However, details of this 'double event' were not released to the public until they were published in the newspapers on Monday 1 October.

It has been assumed that only the killer could have known that he had not been able to finish the 'victim off' and had not had enough time to 'clip her ears'. Together with the 'Dear Boss' letter, this postcard has also become iconic in the portrayal of 'Jack the Ripper'.

It was taken more seriously than other letters because of the short window between the murders and the time the postcard was sent. The police took these two texts seriously enough to produce and post copies outside of police stations on 3 October, 1888. Following this, on 4 October, the two texts were also published in many newspapers, even though some had obtained the information already by 1 October.

Besides these two texts delivered to the Central News Agency, a large number of other letters and postcards were sent to several other recipients such as the press and the police between October and November 1888.

The most common theory about the authorship of these two texts is that journalists fabricated them to increase newspaper sales. Modern analysis carried out on these two texts established linguistic evidence supporting the hypothesis that the two had been written by the 'same person'.

The results of this analysis constitute new forensic evidence in the 'Jack the Ripper' case. However, they don't reveal information about the identity of the killer.

Source: Andrea Nini: 'An Authorship Analysis of the Jack the Ripper Letters' in *Digital Scholarship in the Humanities,* vol 33, Issue 3, September 2018, pp. 621-636.

The name 'Jack the Ripper' gathered some support because of the accuracy of that name being synonymous with the horrendous details of the victims' injuries. Although the first letter was later uncovered as a hoax, the world's press seized on this sensational name. The view taken by the Metropolitan Police was that they were the creation of an enterprising journalist. Without any evidence to the contrary, we must now accept that they were hoaxes.

The Main Police Suspects for the Killings

The identity of the Whitechapel killer has been hotly debated ever since the events in 1888. There have been over 100 suspects having been suggested. While many theories have been proffered, some more advanced than others, none of them have proved to be convincing.

Some of these theories have suggested that the killer was a medical doctor, possibly even an educated upper-class individual who ventured into the seedy Whitechapel district for experience of what was on offer there.

While this may be plausible, the notion of such an individual being the 'Ripper' draws essentially upon cultural perceptions. These include a fear of the medical profession generally, and distrust of modern science or the exploitation of the poor by the rich. Many perceived the 'Ripper' as a common worker, possibly a butcher or other tradesman who lived locally and was employed during the week. This provided an explanation for why the murders occurred on or near the weekend.

There appears to be overwhelming agreement that the 'Ripper' was essentially local to the Whitechapel district of East London. The following suspects are those who were 'favoured' by the police officers conducting the murder investigations. However, there remains a glaring lack of substantial evidence to link any of these individuals to the crimes. Yet each of them had attracted suspicion from the more senior ranks of the Metropolitan Police.

[1] Montague John Druitt

Druitt was born in Wimborne Minster, Dorset, on 15 August, 1857, the second son of surgeon William Druitt. At the age of 13, he won a scholarship to Winchester College. He was an accomplished cricketer and debater, and in 1876, he was awarded a Winchester Scholarship to New College, Oxford. He left Oxford in 1860 and was employed as an assistant schoolmaster at a private school in Blackheath, London. He decided to read for the Bar and was admitted to the Inner Temple in May 1882, finding chambers at 9, Kings' Bench Walk, in the Temple. Druitt was named as a 'Ripper' suspect by the Assistant Chief Constable of the Metropolitan Police CID, Sir Melville Macnaghten. He was last seen alive on Monday 3 December 1888 and his body was recovered from the Thames on 31 December.

It has been suggested that the inclusion of Druitt as a suspect was based on the unquestioning acceptance of the prevailing theory that 'Jack the Ripper' committed suicide after the final killing of Mary Jane Kelly. Interestingly, this was the only suspicion not shared by the police as a whole. It lay entirely in Macnaghten's own conviction that Druitt was involved in the killings.

The cause of death relating to Druitt was given as 'suicide by drowning'. Because his suicide occurred just weeks after the murder of Mary Kelly, this prompted the police to consider him as a prime suspect. However, after further investigation, the only thing that seemed to link Druitt to the murders was the coincidental timing of his suicide.

It appears that shortly before Druitt's death, he was dismissed from the Blackheath school. It has been suggested that this was related to the suggestion that he might have been involved in alleged homosexual practices, although there was nothing to substantiate this allegation. However, this in itself may very well have been enough to drive Druitt to suicide.

On Saturday morning of the 8 December 1888, some six hours after the estimated time of the killing of Annie Chapman, Druitt was playing cricket for Blackheath Club. Also, on Saturday 1 September, the day following the killing of Mary Ann Nichols, the first of the five murders, Druitt was in Dorset again playing cricket. His home at the time was in Kent, miles away from Whitechapel. Most experts agree that the killer had to be local to Whitechapel.

Later in the investigations into the spate of killings, Detective Inspector Frederick Abberline of Scotland Yard CID dismissed Druitt as a serious suspect, due to a lack of any substantial new evidence, beyond that of the 'coincidental suicide'. In addition, it could not be conclusively proved that Druitt had any connection with the Whitechapel area of London.

[2] Severin Klosowski (Alias George Chapman)

Polish-born Klosowski emigrated to the UK just before the start of the 'Ripper' murders, probably between 1887 and 1888. It does appear that around 1893-4, he changed his name to Chapman, and in 1903, he was executed for the poisoning of three of his wives. He worked as a butcher in Whitechapel during the period of the murders.

It is believed that Abberline favoured Klosowski above all the others suspects. However, he has been dismissed as a serious suspect mainly due to his Modus Operandi or MO. This was overwhelmingly poisoning and not 'butchering' his victims.

[3] Aaron Kosminski

Kosminski was an insane Polish-Jew who was admitted to the County Lunatic Asylum at Colney Hatch, London, in 1891. He came to England in 1882 and was unmarried. His occupation was a hairdresser in Whitechapel during the period of the Ripper killings. It has been suggested, mainly by social historians of this period, that the reason why Kosminski was included in the police investigation was because he had become a victim of growing anti-Semitism in the East End of London following the killings. In July 1890, he was admitted to Mile End Town Workhouse, where he was regarded as being able-bodied but insane. In February 1891, he was declared to be 'of unsound mind' and he was committed to the County Lunatic Asylum at Coney Heath, London, where he remained for three years before being admitted to another asylum in 1894, dying there in March 1919.

[4] John Pizer

Pizer was arrested by PS William Thicke on 10 September, 1888, following the murders of Mary Ann Nichols and Annie Chapman. He became known in the area as 'Leather Apron' presumably because of his trade. He was a Polish Jew who worked as a bootmaker in Whitechapel. He was believed by PS Thicke to have committed a number of minor assaults on prostitutes in the area.

Although the investigating officer in the early stages of the murder inquiries believed that there was no evidence against Pizer, many locals suspected him of being the 'Ripper'. He was later cleared of suspicion when it was discovered that he had alibis for the two killings. He had been staying with relatives at the time of one of the killings, and talking with a police constable while watching a raging fire on the London docks at the time of the other killing.

Pizer, having known Sergeant Thicke for years, claimed that he had been detained by him as a result of Thicke's animosity towards him, rather than as the result of any substantial evidence linking him to any of the killings. Although he did have a previous conviction for a stabbing offence, there was no substantial evidence to suggest that Pizer was the 'Ripper'. Being absolved from any suspicions of guilt, Pizer was able to obtain monetary compensation from at least one media source that had linked his name to the Whitechapel murders.

[5] Francis Tumblety

Tumblety was an Irish-American who made a small fortune posing as an 'Indian Herbal Doctor', travelling throughout the United States and Canada. He was also perceived as a 'woman-hating quack'.

It was well known that Tumblety despised all women but particularly prostitutes. This hatred was put down to an earlier marriage to a woman whom he later discovered was leading a double life, as both a wife and a prostitute.

It is reported that Tumblety hosted an all-male dinner party in Washington DC in which he displayed his own personal collection of preserved female reproductive organs. He also boasted that they had come from every class of woman. It comes as no surprise that this claim came to the attention of law enforcement agencies in the USA.

It appears that in 1865, Tumblety was arrested for complicity in the Abraham Lincoln assassination, but he was later released without charge. In 1869, the 36-year-old 'doctor' visited Ireland and then England, staying at the Langham Hotel in London.

In 1874, Tumblety appeared to have settled in Liverpool, setting up his herbal business there. During this time, he did make frequent visits back to the USA and then returning to England in 1878, visiting London at least twice a year. He did set up an office in London in the 1880s. It is known that he was in the City on Friday 31 August, which coincided with the murder of Mary Ann Nichols in Buck's Row, Whitechapel.

On that same day, Tumblety committed an act of 'gross indecency' with another man in London. It also appears that this was not his first detected act of that nature.

Again, on Sunday, 14 October, he was caught out again indulging in the same activity. Then on Friday, 2 November 1888, the week before the final murder of Mary Ann Kelly, he was caught again indulging in the same activity.

On Wednesday, 7 November, Tumblety was arrested by the Metropolitan Police on gross indecency charges and appeared at Marlborough Street Police Court. He was remanded on bail for the sum of £300. It appears that between the 20 and 24 of November, Tumblety skipped bail and fled to France. Then on the 24 November, under an alias of Frank Towns for New York.

The oddest thing in connection with Tumblety, is the noticeable absence of his name, not only from newspapers but also from all the official documents which have now become available for public reference. The gravity of the police error in granting Tumblety bail cannot be underestimated. They had him within their reach but let him go.

Under such circumstances, what could have been more damaging for Scotland Yard than the loss of a prime suspect? This error would have demolished the reputations of senior officers. Not entirely surprising, this was certainly a time for a complete 'cover-up'. Detectives investigating Tumblety's movements considered him dangerous enough to pursue him to New York, yet, there is no surviving official record of such pursuit.

On his previous visits to London, Tumblety had usually stayed in hotels. Yet after his return in 1888, he changed his routine and took to lodgings at 22 Batty Street, St George's-in-the-East, right in the heart of *'Ripperland'*. This was obviously a safe 'base' which provided him with easy access to the 'killing field'. In the early hours of Monday, 1 October 1888, shortly after the killings of Elizabeth Stride and Catherine Eddowes, the landlady of the lodging, a German woman, Mrs Kuer, was disturbed by the late return of the 'American gentleman, a doctor who had engaged one of her rooms'.

In the morning, the landlady, who had become suspicious of her lodger told her husband to check the lodger's room. He opened it and found inside a black bag. On opening it, he found a long sharp knife and a pair of blood-stained shirt cuffs. By the very next day, the lodger had left and never returned.

It is not known whether the landlady reported the findings to the police at this stage. It was only later identified that the 'American doctor' was, in fact, Tumblety. It has been suggested that Tumblety had been occupied in the early hours of 1 October at around 1:40am in Mitre Square, killing Catherine Eddowes. It took 10-15 minutes to walk there from Batty Street. Tumblety must have realised that the police would move rapidly on his lodgings after the Mitre Square murder.

It was revealed that in October 1888, Scotland Yard had contacted the San Francisco Police requesting a sample of Timblety's handwriting which they did receive. *The New York Times* of 19 November 1888, reported the arrest of Tumblety in London on the 7 November, but on suspicion of complicity in the Whitechapel murders, which was incorrect. There was nothing to indicate that his arrest was in connection with anything other than the gross indecency charges. What this article does indicate is that the London CID did not have sufficient evidence to charge Tumblety with the murders.

On Sunday, 2 December 1888, Tumblety arrived back in New York. Two detectives from the New York Police Department had been detailed to keep surveillance on him. Chief Inspector Thomas Byrne of the Detective Bureau of the NYPD, stated that there was no charge whatever against Tumblety. He had him followed for the sole purpose of securing details of his temporary address. It was also pointed out to Scotland Yard that Tumblety could not be arrested for there was no proof of his complicity in the Whitechapel murders and the crime for which he was on bail in England (gross indecency) was not extraditable.

It does appear that a detective had been sent over to America from Scotland Yard as soon as it was realised that Tumblety was on the run. It appears that in 1901, Tumblety was in Baltimore, and in 1903 he died in St John's Charity Hospital in St Louis.

'Dr' Tumblety's personal characteristics and behaviour patterns do present a series of 'coincidences', which would seem to defy mere chance. He had a most virulent hatred of women in general and prostitutes in particular. He boasted of his collection of female organs, and he used aliases. He was in London at the material times of the killings. He had been the subject of police inquiry prior to his arrest. After his arrest and flight to America, the murders ceased.

However, many experts of the Ripper case have dismissed Tumblety due to his appearance and age, which did not match anyone described by witnesses. Even with a series of 'coincidences' that appear convincing, there was no firm evidence that connected him to the actual killings.

Due in large part to London's evening newspaper, *The Star*, founded in 1888, the Ripper murders were highly publicised and sensationalised. In addition, the police were very careful to conceal what few clues they did have from the 'snooping' media.

This obviously resulted in a lot of speculation as to who might be responsible for the murders. This prompted the hungry media to propose a list of possible suspects based entirely upon public opinion and popular local suspicions.

In 1888, Police Science (Forensics) was in its infancy. Protection and examination of a crime scene is the most basic step at the beginning of any criminal investigation. Even in 1888, the need for preserving the crime scene was understood.

Many clues can be gleaned from the position of a victim's body, items found close to the body, and the condition of the ground surrounding the scene. All these factors are of importance to an investigation.

By allowing bystanders to wander around a crime scene, as was the practice then, vital evidence such as footwear impressions or blood flow patterns could be destroyed. Any of these things can easily cause an investigation to look in the wrong direction for the offender.

By the end of the Ripper killing spree in November 1888, the police were more conscientious about crime scene preservation. Miller's Court, the last crime scene after the killing of Mary Jane Kelly, was kept secure from the public. However, this was the only crime scene out of the five that was 'indoors', so preserving this scene was not as much a problem as those before.

Once a crime scene is secure, a thorough search should be conducted. The most critical need during this time is light. A few small lanterns or torches are insufficient to be able to conduct a detailed crime scene search. However, the art of searching a crime scene is one aspect that has not changed over the years. The investigator simply looks for anything that does not appear to be present at the scene naturally. Something that could have been used during the commission of the crime itself.

At the crime scene of the killing of Mary Kelly, a hatchet is believed to have been present in the victim's room at Miller's Court. If so, its presence appears to have been ignored because there is no reference to such an item in either the police or medical reports. This could also be because of the common knowledge that the Ripper used a very sharp knife to carry out his mutilations.

During the period of the Whitechapel killings, there were numerous people in Whitechapel engaged in investigating the murders – in addition to the police themselves. There were the newspaper reporters, private detectives, vigilance committee members, and all combined to seek information. Rumours were in abundance, and reports of suspicious characters were common, with mobs of scared and angry people chasing anyone who did not seem to look right.

At night, police were stationed close together to see and hail one another using their whistles. They had orders to stop and question anyone seen out after midnight. It is reasonable to assume that during times of heightened vigilance, there would be many 'field' interviews conducted by the police. It is also reasonable to believe that the Ripper himself was interviewed at some point during this time.

Obviously, he provided a satisfactory explanation that allowed him to go about his business in the area. What is important here is that there was no written record made of any of these 'field' interviews for later comparison. This could possibly have led to identifying a suspect. Today, 'field' interviews are conducted on the streets by detectives and constables every day, and number more than are undertaken formally. Just talking to someone about a certain crime constitutes an 'investigative interview'. Therefore, it is vitally important that each and every one of these is documented in writing.

With what is known about the Ripper's style of killing, it seems unlikely that there would be any 'defence wounds' on the victims. When a person is strangled to the point of unconsciousness or death before the wounding begins, they have no opportunity to put up their hands and attempt to deflect the blows. The police cannot be blamed for failing to apprehend the Ripper because they were handicapped by their methods, not by their genuine desire to achieve a result.

The police did recognise that the killings were linked and were likely to be the work of one man. However, once they reached that conclusion, they did not follow through by combining departmental efforts to pursue their target.

Today, the police faced with a similar serial killer would establish a joint 'task force' with all concerned departments assigning officers to work on the case as a 'unit'. Without such combination of forces, information one department collected could easily be missed by another.

Today, even when using all available techniques and technology, there is no guarantee of capturing any given criminal. Often a police force investigating a series of murders is put in the unfortunate position of having to wait for another murder to occur, even knowing that this will cost another life. The hope is that on the next occasion, the killer will make a mistake or leave clues to his identity.

The best-case scenario that modern forensic science and investigative procedures could have provided the London Police in 1888 would be the ability to eliminate certain information and suspects from further scrutiny in the absence of hard evidence suggesting their involvement. Eliminating information that proved irrelevant would have allowed them to spend more time investigating clues that may have led eventually to the capture of The Ripper.

Following the police investigation of the Ripper killings, some critics have raised the question of whether the London Police were incompetent in their investigation. It is a fact that the police attempts to bring the Ripper to justice did end in failure. However, it should be remembered that modern criminal detection techniques were not available to the police at that time.

Whilst the investigation certainly had its flaws, the police did as much as they could, lacking the many modern forensic aids we take for granted today. In 1888, 'forensic' science as a distinct specialism did not form an integral part of crime investigation. For us today, being well acquainted with this science thanks to such TV programmes as *CSI* and *Silent Witness,* the use of photography and video recording is widely seen as vital to any murder investigation.

At the time of the Whitechapel killings, photography hardly rated as an 'essential' element in an investigation. It was considered so unimportant that only one of the Ripper's victims, Mary Kelly, was actually photographed *in situ* at the crime scene.

However, by 1888, both the Metropolitan and City of London Police were employing the services of local freelance photographers to record the bodies of those who had died suddenly as a means of establishing positive identification. In the killing of Catherine Eddowes, it does appear that the City of London Police were more advanced than their Metropolitan counterparts in recording the immediate crime scene. They also made sketches of the area which could be used at the subsequent Inquest into the victim's death.

As regards the crime scenes of the other victims, little was done to make a photographic record of the bodies prior to removal to the mortuary. The main concern of the initial police investigations was to remove the bodies from the scene as quickly as possible. Many writers of the case believe that the London Police missed apprehending the killer for the simple reason that they were looking for the wrong sort of suspect.

The early theories of criminology in 1888 pointed to a 'dribbling lunatic' as the perpetrator of these killings. Therefore, the overriding consideration guiding the police inquiries centred upon 'medical skill and insanity'. Understandably, DNA analysis was completely irrelevant to solving the identity of the killer as were most other forms of physical evidence we rely on today. For example, fingerprinting was only introduced into Scotland Yard in 1902. Investigators were limited to circumstantial evidence such as a number of conflicting witness statements. The closest thing investigators had to forensic evidence were the observations of the police surgeons from examining the crime scene and from the results of the victims' post-mortem examinations.

Immediately a body was discovered by the police, the appointed police surgeon for the division would be called to attend the scene. They were responsible for determining when and how the victim had died. They would also take notes of any belongings or objects of interest at the crime scene. They would examine wounds inflicted on the victims and use their observations to determine what weapons would have been used to inflict the injuries.

The most difficult task facing the police surgeon then and today was to determine the time of death with any certainty. Quite often, their decisions often conflicted with those of witness testimony and even police theories.

The police surgeons involved in the investigation of the Whitechapel killings also conducted the post-mortem examinations in addition to their regular duties. This is in contrast to the position today where a police surgeon would carry out the initial examination and confirm death at the scene, then refer the body to a forensic pathologist for further investigation to determine the cause of death.

In 1888, the police surgeon would produce a report detailing all that was found at the crime scene to record the wounds visible from the outside of the body and then a detailed summary of the post-mortem findings.

All the Inquests into the deaths of the five Whitechapel killings ended with the same conclusions: "death by person or persons unknown".

Even today, with all the genetic and molecular biology applications available, a surprising number of serial killers manage to avoid detection. One reason for this shortcoming is *'linkage blindness'*, where patterns of crimes are not recognised by investigators. For example, in the 'Ripper' killings, the absence of a struggle with his victims demonstrates both pre-planning and prior experience on the part of the killer.

This planning was also revealed in his choice of public murder locations. This allowed him to conduct his crimes largely undetected and then disappear unnoticed. The *geographical* patterns of the attacks carried out by Jack the Ripper indicate some important aspects of the murders. One is that all the killings were clearly circumscribed within a limited area. This suggests that he was very familiar with the area around Whitechapel and that something kept bringing him back that that same locality.

The most obvious reason for this is that he lived within the neighbourhood circumscribed by the locations of the killings. If he did, then it will be necessary to discover why he did not spread his crimes further afield. The criminal who perpetuates a set of killings in a public area is telling us something about his familiarity with that particular place.

There is a truism that "where we go depends upon what we know to be available". Therefore "what we know depends upon where we go". The very distances over which crimes are committed tells us something about the individual responsible for them. In Victorian Whitechapel, it is not that surprising that the Ripper moved around on foot. However, if he did leave the area in, say, a horse-drawn cab, this does not explain that the furthest distance between any two of the crime scenes was within easy walking distance. Whitechapel was not the only area of Victorian London with narrow streets and potential victims. This would suggest that the locations of the Ripper crimes were well within walking distance of each other. He could walk to them from where he had a base or home. It is to an examination of the modern techniques of *Geographical and Offender Profiling*, applied to the Whitechapel killings, that we turn to in Chapter Three.

Chapter Three: Geographical And Psychological Profiles Of The Whitechapel Murders

In general, the process of criminal investigation has changed very little since the Whitechapel killings in 1888. There is still the basic process of identifying suspects, tracing them, and deciding whether to examine them more closely or to eliminate them from the investigation.

However, there are obvious differences of approach available today, which were not available to the police in 1888. Evidence is much more carefully collected and analysed today. The various branches of science; physics, chemistry, biology and pathology, all contribute to the interpretation of evidence, cause of death, and other information gathered from the available evidence. For the person in charge of the investigation, key aspects of any suspect are crucial. These may include their having the opportunity to commit the crime in the first place, and how that fits in with what is already known about a particular suspect's *'modus operandi'* or MO. These are the distinctive actions taken by the offender which link his crimes together - and link him to the crimes.

Where an offender operates is one of the most distinctive features of that person's crimes. It is of great value for any investigation. It can direct house-to-house inquiries and also narrow down suspects. The task of linking crimes is vitally important to investigators. By tying an offender to a number of crimes, more information then becomes available about that offender's criminal actions. Consequently, a major management decision has to be made as to whether or not to treat the investigation as one major interconnected or serial inquiry.

The decision to link crimes is a serious one, and hard forensic evidence is the preferred basis for setting up such an investigation of serial killings. A serial killer kills primarily for a compulsive and quite often sexual reason or the pure love and need for killing itself.

In the case of the murder of prostitutes, detectives are daunted by the possibility that one of their anonymous clients could be responsible. This involves a wide field of possible suspects, many of whom it is virtually impossible to trace. However, it is hard to imagine any circumstances under which a casual anonymous client would inflict horrendous injuries on a woman, irrespective of their status. Detectives generally believe that it is within a relationship that violence against prostitutes is most likely to burst out to a vicious level rather than attacks by clients.

There is another alternative explanation: the determination to silence a potential witness. However, even in such circumstances, it would not be expected to result in horrendous mutilation of the victim.

The world in which both male and female prostitutes live is extremely difficult for police to penetrate. Consequently, many unsolved murders include people who sell their bodies for gain. Any act against another person is committed on a wave of emotion. Different kinds and degrees of emotion will be reflected in different forms of actions. Consequently, the number of stabs, vicious thrusts, the severing of the head, all of these provide a mixture of messages. For example, the wild frenzy of a murder reveals a mixture of approaches to the act of murder itself.

This raises two pertinent questions; was the attacker a person with wild mood swings exemplified in his attack? Frenzy followed by remorse? Or did the attack itself display different styles or approaches? If so, this would indicate that more than one person was involved in the killing.

It has been found that many of the 'qualitative' aspects of murder have been described as 'disorganised'. The violence and mutilations inflicted on a victim, as well as leaving the body at the scene, are regarded as hallmarks of this type of murderer. The criminal who reveals 'confusion' in his attacks is less likely to be a person who actively searches for his victims and more likely to be an 'opportunist'.

One of the firmest hypotheses about a criminal's actions is that knowledge of and familiarity with a particular area are prerequisites for many violent crimes. The committing of a violent crime near an offender's base or home by an 'impulsive' person will indicate that it was not his first crime. His other crime would be considered to be the first crime, and is likely to have occurred in a familiar location in some general area.

It is the actual offence itself which is the focus of all subsequent criminal activity. In particular, crimes against people as opposed to property crime, will include a very careful consideration of the victim(s) themselves. It is general practice for a police murder inquiry to move outwards from the victim to relatives, friends and neighbours, until a network of contacts reveals a more clear picture on which to focus police attention.

The area in which crimes are committed, the type of victim, and many other aspects of an attack, are generally quite consistent for any one offender. For any violent attack, there will be numerous aspects of the offence that need to be considered. Serial killers are not random in their actions. They have a mode of acting which includes how they find their victims and what they inflict upon them. To this end, such killings are premeditated or planned over a period of time. They are not impulsive actions.

The significance of the place in which the killing takes place is especially important. Investigators often discover that the offender has some affinity to a particular location. Consequently, the most objective and observable aspect of any crime is where it happens, and such places are not without significance in any murder investigation.

Criminals can choose literally anywhere to commit their crimes, and this will be reflected in the size of the geographical range over which they operate. The use of crime locations to understand an offender, and to suggest where they may have a base for operating, is known today as the *Geographical Profiling* of crime.

An offender's journey to crime has two specific features which are particularly relevant to serial killers. The first is the way in which a home or base acts as a focus for their criminal activity. The second is the geographical 'scale' over which their criminal activities are committed. This base helps to form an observable pattern of criminal activity. This scale can be limited, for those who are very local and seeking opportunities within walking distance from their base. It can also include those offenders who travel further afield to commit their crimes.

This poses the question; what creates a dependable pattern of criminal activity which is consistent? The answer to this question must be where there are the opportunities for crime, where there are known victims, and where there is ready and easy access and escape. All these factors will shape the patterns of an offender's behaviour. If an offender's predilections are for a particular type of victim, such as prostitutes, then they will be drawn to locations in which these people are readily available.

The significance of the place in which the crime is committed is especially important in the crime of serial killing. Was it indoors or outdoors? Was it a place open to the public or private? What is the typical pattern of activity associated with the specific location?

The seriousness of the offences influences the resources employed on an investigation, together with the initial information gathered by investigators. It is necessary to establish a distinction between 'pre-meditated' and 'non-

THE WHITECHAPEL MURDERS - LOCATIONS

SHOREDITCH

⑤ MILLERS COURT. 9.11.88

② HANBURY STREET. 8.9.88

① BUCK'S ROW 31.8.88

COMMERCIAL STREET

WHITECHAPEL ROAD

④ MITRE SQUARE. 30.9.88

ALDGATE HIGH STREET

COMMERCIAL ROAD

WHITECHAPEL ③ BERNER STREET. 30.9.88

premeditated' crimes to understand the offender's behaviour. For a series of violent crimes, premeditation presupposes choices on the part of the offender; victim, place, time and possibly the route to follow in reaching and leaving the crime scene. In pre-meditated acts, the offender is drawn by the crime.

This concept is crucial because it reflects a 'logical, calculated' behaviour on the part of the offender.

In contrast to pre-meditated actions, 'opportunistic' crimes are more influenced by external factors without a specific choice of victim or target. Consequently, in opportunistic situations, places, times and targets, are 'randomly' selected.

Distinguishing between pre-meditated and opportunistic crimes are essential when considering the application of geographical profiling to a major crime investigation. The expression 'serial murder' can be defined as 'the unlawful killing of two or more victims, by the same offender in separate incidents'.

In terms of this definition, the Whitechapel murders were definitely 'serial killings'. The serial killer can select his victims in specific categories of society, according to social status in society. Serial murders can be further sub-divided geographically between 'stable' and 'transient'.

In general, 'stable' serial killers live, kill and dispose of their victims in the same area of their criminal activities. The 'transient' killer tends to travel continually from one area to another, and disposes of their victims in unrelated and sometimes distant places.

The Whitechapel Murders of 1888

When reviewing the murder locations of Jack the Ripper there is always the problem (as in many murder investigations) of being absolutely certain which crimes are, in fact, 'linked'. However, it is generally now accepted that there were five victims in the Whitechapel murders known as the *Canonical Five*.

The most relevant point to note is the essentially limited *geographical distribution* of the 'Ripper' killings. This fact raises one important question; why would a man seeking out women available on the streets of Whitechapel limit himself to a relatively small area of activity, which does appear to be the case with the 'Ripper'?

Of course, it could be the prevalence of possible targets. In this case, a familiarity with, and the reputation of the area, could easily combine to draw the offender to

Whitechapel. It is the *spatial distribution* of the crime locations which reveal that the killer had some familiarity with the area. This also suggests that he either lived within that area or travelled into it from outside regularly. If we consider the locations of the 'Ripper' killings, the geographical distribution of the crime locations clearly demonstrates how localised they really were. The victims were encountered and then murdered in locations that were within close proximity to each other. In addition, these locations where the bodies were discovered indicate that the places had some significance for the killer.

The first murder of Mary Ann Nichols was in Buck's Row, Whitechapel, on Friday, 31 August 1888. This crime location marks out the eastern-most limit to the area covering the five murders and can be regarded as defining an eastern boundary to the 'geographical range' over which the whole murders took place. Obviously, after this first murder, the killer would need to avoid detection by not revisiting this area too soon after the event.

The second murder took place on Saturday, 8 September in the back yard of 29, Hanbury Street, Spitalfields, the victim being Annie Chapman. Of particular significance, the location of this second murder was approximately one mile in distance from that of the Mary Ann Nichols murder scene, but in a westerly direction.

As would be expected, these first two killings aroused public outcry and fear and would also attract police activity and surveillance. The killer would now have to exercise more caution if he was to continue with his activities. As a consequence of this, there was a noticeable gap of three weeks before the Ripper struck once again.This has often been regarded as a 'cooling-off' period.

The third killing – of Elizabeth Stride on Sunday, 30 September – occurred in the passageway between numbers 40 and 42, Berner Street, Whitechapel. Again, the crime location of this killing was approximately one mile from that of the first murder in Buck's Row but in a southerly direction.

Having now committed a total of three killings which marked out a triangle of offences, this would suggest that the Ripper is now limited in the range over which he can operate safely. His paramount need is to avoid those places where he may be recognised or be drawn to the attention of the police. Viewing the sketch map, it can be seen that the only place he has not visited is the south-west corner of his activity range.

In the early hours of Sunday 30 September, the very same day as the killing of Elizabeth Stride, the 'Ripper' struck again. On this occasion, the location was Mitre Square, lying just within the boundary of the City of London.

Significantly, this location was again, approximately one mile south of Hanbury Street, the scene of the killing of Catherine Eddowes. This would suggest that the Ripper was moving back to a more preferred location which would also allow him to maintain a 'safe distance' of around three-quarters of a mile between each crime location.

Having now committed four killings, the Ripper had mapped out the four corners of an area encompassing the parishes of Shoreditch, Spitalfields and Whitechapel. He was then faced with a major problem. If he was to continue operating under his same regime, he was limited in the opportunities now open to him. Anywhere within his defined area of 'criminal activity' would be less than a 'safe distance' from any one of his previous crime scenes. One option available to him is for him to move out of the area altogether. However, this has problems of its own. If he was not familiar with the other surrounding areas of the East End of London, he was forced to remain in the Whitechapel and Spitalfields areas.

With this in mind, it would be reasonable to

predict that the Ripper's next move would be in close proximity to one of his previous murder locations. After a break in activity for about one month, he did strike again. On Friday, 9 November, Mary Jane Kelly was murdered in her room at 13, Miller's Court, Dorset Street, Spitalfields. This last killing was less than one mile distance north of his fourth murder in Mitre Square.

These five crime locations marked out a rough 'circle' of criminal activity ascribed to the Ripper. In addition, if we consider the chronological sequence of the murders, they reveal a tendency to move towards the western side of Whitechapel.

The two killings that occurred on the same day, (30 September) are of particular significance to the geographic aspects of these murders. They also raise the question; were these two murders committed by the Ripper on his way out from his base, or on his return to base?

It would be reasonable to assume that the killer was on his way back from having committed the first killing of Elizabeth Stride in Berner Street, Whitechapel, because of its location in respect to Mitre Square, the scene of the next killing of Catherine Eddowes on the same evening. It can be further assumed that on his return journey after the murder of Elizabeth Stride, he saw the opportunity to commit another killing, the murder of Catherine Eddowes. Consequently, the second killing of the evening in Mitre Square would be nearer to his home base.

The Timings of the Killings

It was estimated that the murder of the first victim, Mary Ann Nichols, occurred about 3:40am on the 31 September. Should we regard this as late at night or early in the morning? It would be expected that a crime committed late at night would be located furthest away from the offender's base. In this case, he would be moving out from his base, searching for suitable victims.

This would have taken him into the early hours of the morning, before locating a victim, killing her and escaping largely unseen. The attack on Mary Nichols could be seen as late into the night and as far away as possible from his base.

If we make a further assumption that Buck's Row, the location of the first killing, was some distance from the offender's base, this would confirm the view that the journey from Berner Street after the murder of Elizabeth Stride to Mitre Square, and the killing of Catherine Eddowes, was on his way back to his base.

Elizabeth Stride was murdered around 2:00am, and Catherine Eddowes at about 2:45am. It has been suggested that the first of these killings was at the end of his search, and having been disturbed, the killer was returning to his base when he encountered Catherine Eddowes, his fourth victim. Taking the timing of the other two murders, the second killing of Annie Chapman, this was estimated to be just before 6:00am.

Again, it can be suggested that the killer was on his way out from his base early in the morning. He was likely to be seeking a victim close to his base. Alternatively, it could also mean that the killer was on his way back to his base after completing an 'all-night-search' before finding an opportunity for another 'kill'.

In the final killing of Mary Jane Kelly inside her room at Miller's Court, it is more difficult to ascertain the timing of with any certainty. Although her body was not discovered until around 10:45am, there were indications that it was likely that she had been killed a few hours earlier, according to the medical evidence. This would make the timing of the murder similar to that of Annie Chapman in Hanbury Street, Spitalfields.

These timings pose two relevant questions. Would the killer risk being far from his base at a time when the area was becoming crowded with people at the start of the day? Or would that time of day be precisely the time when the killer would be out and about at the furthest point from his base?

Reviewing all the evidence of the crime scenes, together with the approximate timings of the killings, it would be reasonable to speculate that an area around Miller's Court and Mitre Square could possibly be the closest to the Ripper's base. Also, the timings of the murders are consistent with him wanting to be nearer to the west of Whitechapel, rather than the east, once his killings have been accomplished.

However, if the killer is clearly targeting a particular type of criminal opportunity, then the chances will decrease because it is the opportunity for the crime which will determine where he will offend, rather than the location of his base. However, there is still the real possibility that 'Jack' came into the area precisely because of the opportunities available for him to carry out his intended series of killings.

However, the distribution of the crime locations offers the real possibility that he did have a base within the proscribed area of the killings. If we assume that 'Jack' did have a base within the area covered by the crime locations, we have available various forms of analysis which can be applied to try to locate this base. One such analysis is to ensure that the crimes describe a region of activity spreading out from the base. On this assumption, the base would be located towards the middle of a hypothetical 'circle' encompassing all the known crime locations. Another approach would be to draw horizontal lines coming from the four furthest crime scenes inwards. Where all these lines converge, this could indicate the possible base of the offender.

Of course, the predictions must take into account other factors such as modes of transport available for the killer. However, in the case of an offender seeking opportunities for crime closer to his base, his area of criminal activity will be more confined to a specific range. There is always the possibility that 'Jack' had a base outside of his 'killing field' and did travel into the Whitechapel area seeking out specific targets. His frequent visits to the area would have made him familiar with the layout of the area. On this point, it is difficult to be completely certain.

However, given the level of knowledge required to move around an area at night with the confidence displayed by the Ripper, it is highly unlikely that these were based on regular, fleeting visits into the area. It is more plausible that he had walked the streets of Whitechapel many times, even before instigating his reign of terror.

A Comparable Case: The 'Yorkshire Ripper'

Between July 1975 and November 1980, there was a series of brutal attacks on women which were believed to be the work of the same individual. There was a total of twenty attacks, thirteen of which resulted in the deaths of the victims. These attacks occurred within Yorkshire and Lancashire in the north of England.

This series of attacks proved very difficult for the police to investigate. They did not have sufficient forensic evidence to link the crimes, and the spread of the offences over a relatively wide geographical area made it difficult for them to decide where to focus their attention.

Some of the twenty victims were prostitutes working the streets of northern cities like Bradford, Leeds and Manchester. However, these victims also included women in other occupations.

The offender attacked them with a hammer and a screwdriver, inflicting horrendous injuries on his victims. It was this method of attack that earned him the nickname, The Yorkshire Ripper. Seven of his victims did survive to identify their attacker.

    The Yorkshire Ripper's first attack was in July 1975 in the West Yorkshire town of Keighley. This was followed a few weeks later by another attack in Halifax. These were classed as 'attempted murder'.

    Then in October of 1975, he murdered a young woman in Leeds. These first three attacks, while being a dozen or so miles from each other, did mark out a pattern of offending behaviour. Between January 1976 and June 1977, the offender committed a further five murders, four of which were centred on the city of Leeds.

    The Yorkshire Ripper struck again in July 1977 in Bradford, resulting in the attempted murder of a woman. Then, from October 1977 through to November 1980, the offender committed seven further murders and six attempted murders.

    The movements of the offender made it clear that he had access to a vehicle. He was also familiar with a number of cities in the north of England, and therefore had legitimate reasons to visit them. It was those reasons that enabled him to avoid detection. If he had a vehicle, then he probably used this for his work, which would probably involve him in visiting these different places. This being the case, then these visits would not appear out of the ordinary and therefore not attract undue attention from the police.

    It turned out that the offender, Peter Sutcliffe, was employed as a truck delivery driver. He was a criminal for whom travelling was his Modus Operandi. He also had easy access to modes of transport.

    This case of The Yorkshire Ripper reflects in many ways that of the Whitechapel murders in 1888. Between 1975 and 1981, the residents of Yorkshire and Lancashire were terrorised by a serial killer whom the press had given full attention. The public outcry and panic equalled that experienced in Whitechapel. What is of particular significance are the similarities to the original Ripper killings.

There was one single offender involved, a series of five ritual killings, the majority of the victims were prostitutes, the murders occurred within a proscribed area, and they were all marked by intense media attention. This was almost a 'replay' of the 1888 crimes. There were even messages to the police purporting to come from the killer himself in the form of 'tape recordings'. These paralleled the *'Dear Boss'* letters of 1888, proving they were most likely, bogus and hoaxes.

The Yorkshire Ripper not only targeted woman the same way as 'Jack' but also killed in a similar way. Although without the same surgical skill of the original Ripper, he mutilated the lower abdomen region of his victims, and in some cases, removed the sex organs from some of his victims.

There was also a 'social' aspect to the habits of both killers. The Chapeltown district of Leeds was, in many ways, very similar to Whitechapel in 1888. It was full of immigrants and was rife with poverty. Both cities boasted a thriving 'red-light' district. In both cases, immigrants were considered suspects or at least targets for the killings. In the Yorkshire Ripper case, the media consistently invoked the example of the legendary Ripper to boost revenues.

In both cases, there is no certainty that the killers were targeting sex workers in particular or just women in general. It is possible that for both men, it was simply women that they abhorred, but that they found sex workers easy targets. This proved true for 'Jack' who was never apprehended.

There was also an assumption that the Yorkshire Ripper targeted sex workers, but he also killed and attacked women of all professions. However, in both cases, it could be said that sex work was simply the scapegoat, and the one thing in common between both killers, was their apparent hatred of women.

After his arrest and trial in 1981, Peter Sutcliffe challenged medical and legal conceptions of 'insanity'. In fact, it was the 'legal' presumption of his insanity that prevailed. Sutcliffe was pronounced guilty on all charges and sentenced to life imprisonment. In March 1984, he was transferred to Broadmoor Secure Hospital for the criminally insane and died there in 2020.

Jack The Ripper': Offender Profile

Criminal profiling, also known as offender profiling or psychological profiling, has become an important method employed by criminal investigators. Profiling helps investigators complete a profile of an unknown and wanted offender and is based on certain characteristics of the offence, such as the style and nature of the crime.

When processing a criminal profile, mainly for murder investigations, there are several stages involved. These will include the collection of all information relating to the physical evidence, photographic evidence, eye witnesses statements and, of course, police incident reports. In the mind of the public and many practitioners, profiling is typical associated with an approach in which the characteristics of the offender are derived from examination and observations of the crime scene itself.

Offender profiling has been referred to as "a technique for identifying the major personality and behavioural characteristics of an individual based on an analysis of the crime he or she has committed".

It has been claimed by experts in this field of psychology that clusters of behaviours can be derived from crime scenes and thereby converted into some taxonomic framework. It has also been argued that the inferential process can be represented by asking the questions, "What to Why to Who?"

Based on crime scene material (what), a particular motivation for the offence behaviour is attributed to the perpetrator (why). This, in turn, leads to the description of the perpetrator's likely characteristics (who). However, 'offender profiling' rests on the assumption that at least certain offenders have consistent behavioural traits. This consistency is thought to persist from crime to crime. It also affects various non-criminal aspects of the offender's personality and lifestyle. This makes them, to some extent, identifiable.

In terms of consistency in offence behaviour, a number of studies have shown some evidence that offenders are relatively consistent in their actions. However, what is most revealing about these studies is the finding that individual behaviours are subject to some fluctuation from crime to crime, due to situational influences. The most significant aspect of criminal behaviour consistency, appears to relate primarily to location, with proximity to that location being the most effective element for linking crimes, particularly those of serial killing. One of the first cases in which criminal or offender profiling was used in an investigation was that of Jack the Ripper, the unidentified serial killer.

In 1888, the London doctor, Thomas Bond, became famous for assisting in the post-mortem of the Ripper's final victim, Mary Ann Kelly. Dr Bond was originally called in to analyse the surgical knowledge of the perpetrator of the crime because of the manner in which he removed internal organs from his victims.

As the investigation continued, Dr Bond examined crime scenes in order to analyse the behaviour that was portrayed at the time of the offence, and also the wound patterns. On November 10, 1888, Dr Bond noted that because of the sexual nature of each crime, the offender suffered from some form of rage and hatred of women.

Dr Thomas Bond was a surgeon at Westminster Hospital and Divisional Police Surgeon to the A-Whitehall Division of the Metropolitan Police, and highly regarded by the Assistant Commissioner and Head of the CID Department, Robert Anderson. He was mainly involved in the Whitechapel murders as a consultant. However, he did attend Miller's Court to inspect the body of the Ripper's final victim, Mary Ann Kelly.

He made his observations in the victim's room on the day of her murder. At the request of Assistant Commissioner Anderson, Bond also submitted a general report on the murders of the remaining four other victims. This report was based on Bond's summary of the medical notes written by the other doctors attending the scenes. He was of the opinion that all five murders were, no doubt, committed by the same hand. His general report began:

"In the cases of Nichols, Chapman, Stride and Eddowes, the throats appear to have been cut from left to right. In the last case, that of Kelly, owing to extensive mutilation, it is impossible to say in what direction the fatal cut was made. However, arterial blood was found on the wall in splashes close to where the woman's head must have been lying. All the circumstances surrounding the murders lead me to form the opinion that the women must have been lying down when murdered, and in every case, the throat was cut. In all cases there appears to be no evidence of struggling, and the attacks were probably so sudden and made in such a position that the women could neither resist nor cry out. In the first four cases, the murderer must have attacked from the right side of the

victims. *In the Dorset Street case (Kelly), he must have attacked in front or from the left, as there would be no room for him between the wall, and the part of the bed on which the woman was lying".*
Source: *"Jack the Ripper: The Definitive Casebook"*, Richard Whittington-Egan, (Amberley Publishing, Stroud, 2018, p.61)

Dr Bond's Profile Of The Ripper

"The murderer must have been a man of physical strength and of great coolness and daring. There is no evidence that he had an accomplice. He must, in my opinion, be a man subject to periodical attacks of homicidal and erotic mania. The character of the mutilations indicate that the man may be in a condition sexually that may be called 'satyriasis'. It is of course possible that the homicidal impulse may have developed from a revengeful or brooding condition of the mind, or that religious mania may have been the original disease, but I do not think that either hypothesis are likely.

The murderer in external appearance is quite likely to be a quiet, inoffensive-looking man, probably middle-aged and neatly and respectably dressed. I think he must be in the habit of wearing a cloak or overcoat or he could hardly have escaped notice in the streets if the blood on his hands or clothes were visible. Assuming the murderer to be such a person, as I have described, he would probably be solitary and eccentric in his habits, also he is most likely to be a man without a regular occupation, but with some small pension or income. He is probably living among respectable persons who have some knowledge of his character and habits and who may have grounds for suspicion that he is not quite right in his mind. Such persons would probably be unwilling to communicate suspicions to the police for fear of trouble or notoriety, whereas if there were a prospect of reward, it might

overcome their scruples."
Source: *"The Complete Jack the Ripper"*, Donald Rumbelow, (London, W.H. Allen, 1987, pp. 140-41)

  In his profile, there is nothing to suggest that Dr Bond was drawing on anything other than his professional experience. Essentially, Bond's profile comprises a number of reasonable speculations to form his hypothesis of the Ripper.
  Obviously since no one was convicted for the Whitechapel killings, the accuracy of Bond's profile cannot be established and is, therefore, somewhat speculative. However, it does merit serious consideration, and the possibilities he proposed would probably be acceptable in modern police investigations. The rapid growth of medicine towards the latter decades of the 19th century led doctors to become involved in criminal investigations as 'pathologists'.
  Their work also embraced the treating of the perpetrators of crime, who were regarded by public opinion as either *'mad'* or *'bad'*. By the 1880s, medical officers offered their opinions about the characteristics of an offender based on their own clinical and 'forensic' experience.
  However, in the case of Jack the Ripper, such medical opinion was divided, and no acceptable grounds were put forward as to a secure diagnosis. In fact, the *sanity v insanity* issue continued to divide the medical profession at the time. The following three extract, all from contemporary medical publications, highlight this area of controversy as regards mental health at the time.

  "The theory of a lunatic appears to us to be by no means at present well established. As far as we are aware, homicidal mania is generally characterised by the one single and fatal act, although we grant this may have been led up to by a deep-rooted sense of delusions. It is most

unusual for a lunatic to plan any complicated crime of this kind. Neither, as a rule, does a lunatic take precautions to escape from the consequences of his act. The truth is, that under the circumstances, nobody can do more than hazard a guess as to the probable condition of mind of the perpetrator of these terrible tragedies. Until more evidence is forthcoming, it appears to us to be useless to speculate upon what can only at present be regarded as problematical."
Source: *The Lancet,* 15 September, 1888

"An editorial indicated the inadvisability of jumping to the conclusion that it was an insane murderer who was responsible for the Whitechapel murders. The most important issue from a medical point of view was that of diagnosis. Medicine did not recognise any specific type of mental disorder which had been described as 'homicidal mania'. Eminent psychiatrists such as Henry Maudsley and CH Mare acknowledged the existence of 'forms of impulsive insanity'. Such persons would probably be unwilling to communicate suspicions to the police, whereas if there was a prospect of reward, it might overcome their scruples."
Source: *British Medical Journal,* 22 September, 1888

"On the subject of the murders, the London public has produced a great quantity of egregiously foolish utterances in the different shapes of rumour, comment, and so-called suggestion, that could well have been collected from a similar number of people in any part of the world. It has also, as a matter of course, blamed the police, while at the same time it has doubtless with the best intentions, done probably as much as in it lay to increase the difficulties in the way of detection. All this was to be looked for. It constitutes one of the most formidable difficulties with which the police are confronted in a case of this kind. All the skill and all the effort of a great system of police have utterly failed to connect anyone with a series of atrocious murders committed not in solitary places, but in one of the most densely populated districts of London, not in the recesses of some lonely wood, but in the public streets of the largest city in the world.

It was the very atrocity of the Whitechapel murders that gave rise to the theory of their being the work of a madman. It is not a novel line of reasoning. The mutilation of the bodies of those wretched women in the East London, taken by itself, is no indication whatsoever of insanity on the part of the perpetrator or perpetrators of the deeds. It is said that the hypothesis of insanity as an explanation of these startling crimes, is borne out by the apparent absence of anything like an adequate motive. But this failure is no ground for inferring insanity, and it would be dangerous so to regard it. Apparent absence of motive is no criterion.

The craftiness of the author, or authors, of these deeds is astounding, and the highest tribute to it is the fact that all attempts at detection have been made in vain. There is, first, cool, and deliberate preparation. There is the choice of a class of victims which, of all others, can most readily and as a matter of ordinary course be decoyed away alone to a secluded place of the kind, and a such an hour. The actual execution of his foul purpose must have been swift and dextrous, and shows coolness of hand and steadiness of purpose. Then all traces of the crime must have been removed from the assassin with great skill and foresight. The perfect circumspection which has characterised his subsequent movements, and has secured complete concealment for him hitherto, has been skilful in the extreme, and must have been previously devised. Lastly, the daring shown in the repetition of the atrocities is only to be equated by the caution shown in refraining from any too foolhardy attempt to repeat them when detection was imminent. These things are all markedly in the direction of disproving insanity.

In contrasting the sane crime with the insane, the criminal lays plans for the execution of his designs; time, place and weapons are all suited to his purpose, and when successful, he either flees from the scene, or makes every effort to avoid discovery. The homicidal monomaniac, on the contrary, for the most part, consults none of the usual conveniences of crime, he falls upon the object of his prey often without the proper means of accomplishing his purpose, and perhaps in the presence of a multitude, as if wishing to court observation, and then voluntarily surrenders himself to the authorities."
Source: *The Journal of Jurisprudence,* November, 1888 – Edinburgh

"The year just closing has, in addition to the usual tally of medico-legal experiences, been marked by a series of crimes, (the Whitechapel murders) of unexampled barbarity. Crimes rendered all the more notable by their repetition, and that, too, in a crowded part of the Metropolis, and by the failure hitherto, to detect their diabolical perpetrator. Even yet, the public mind has not recovered from the terror which they occasioned."
Source: *The Lancet,* December, 1888 – Editorial

A Comparative Profile Of 'The Ripper'

In 1988, to mark the centenary of the Ripper murders, two experts from the American FBI in Quantico produced a 'psychological' profile of 'Jack the Ripper'. This was undertaken by two Special FBI Agents, John E Douglas and Robert R Hazelwood. This profile indicated certain features that the two agents believed would be characteristic of the Ripper.

"He would be male and likely to be between 28 and 36 years of age. He would be of low social class and display none of the supposed surgical or anatomical skills. What he performed was really no more than elementary butchery. He was probably in employment, suggested by the murders being committed at weekends, Friday, Saturday and Sunday nights. Because he was able to commit the crimes between midnight and 6:00am, this was indicative of the absence of a family situation. He was likely to be viewed as a 'loner'. It was highly probable that he had come to the attention of the police before the murders occurred. He had been abused as a child, encouraged by his mother. The physical circumstances of his crimes told us that this was someone who could blend in with his surroundings and not cause suspicion or fear on the part of the prostitutes. The mutilations pointed to a mentally disturbed sexually inadequate person, with a lot of generalised rage against women. His 'blitz' style of attack told of personal and social inadequacy".

      Special Agent Douglas was also certain that, as in the case of Peter Sutcliffe, the styled *Yorkshire Ripper*, he would undoubtedly have been interviewed by police in the course of their investigations.

Source: 'The Ripper Project: Modern Science Solving Mysteries of History' in *American Journal of Forensic Medicine and Pathology* Vol 10, No2, (1989)

This profile was based upon the facts relating to the medical and other evidence recorded in 1888. Agent Douglas also suggested that had this profile been available to the police at the time, it would have helped investigators to narrow down their focus to identify the killer.

Psychological Aspects Of The Murders

      How do victims play a role in the lives of their attackers whom they may never see or know? Anyone who has any doubts about the feminist argument that women are treated as objects for the sexual satisfaction of men need only spend a short time with street prostitutes to be convinced how men can use a woman's body as a 'source' to satisfy their appetites without any attempt at contact between them.

The Whitechapel killings and the injuries inflicted on the five victims were ghastly, but their very intensity and variety tell us something. Many of the wounds were far from being a violent random onslaught that may be associated with a 'wild frenzied attack'. How can these attacks be interpreted?

In the case of the first victim, Mary Ann Nichols, 'the throat had been cut, practically severing the woman's head from her body'. Here we see a very specific action that reveals a distinct message.

These were, in fact, real attempts to turn the victim into a *non-person,* to literally remove their personality. This clinical view implies that the victim had some personal or possible emotional significance for the killer. The attack would be an attempt to destroy that significance by destroying those aspects of the body that represent that individual person.

So in this sense, the victim was not just any person as far as the offender was concerned, but in some way special to him. This would suggest some established contact with the victim, a form of familiarity. However, this would be a relationship built upon the victim as a 'body' that could be 'nullified' by the removal of her head.

When investigating the murder of prostitutes, detectives are daunted by the real possibility that one of her many anonymous 'clients' could have committed the murder. This would provide a vast field of potential suspects, many of whom would never be traced.

However, it is difficult to imagine circumstances in which a casual anonymous client would inflict the number and variety of wounds and mutilations found on the five victims of Jack the Ripper. If a client did murder a prostitute in a fit of rage, he would be expected to leave the crime scene as quickly as possible, not linger to inflict more mutilations.

One exception to this expectation would be the rare cases in which the body of the victim was systematically 'ritually' mutilated. It is still firmly believed that the majority of murders happen within some form of relationship, not between apparent strangers. Paying for sex is already a form of power and control. This, in itself, is a form of domination would, under normal circumstances, reduce the need or desire to physically violate the woman. Even if the determination was to silence a potential witness, this would not be expected to produce numerous wounds and mutilations.

Any aggressive act against another person is carried out on an outburst of emotion. Different kinds and degrees of emotion will be reflected in the different kinds of actions carried out. In the Ripper killings, the wild 'frenzy' of the attacks, but the total absence of any personal evidence, reveals a mixture of approaches to the actual act of the killings.

Do these reveal an attacker with wild 'mood swings' during his attacks? Or were the different 'styles' of attack an indication that different people were involved in the killing? On the basis of the medical opinion and evidence, it was generally accepted that the 1888 killings were the work of one individual offender.

Were the wounds and mutilations 'disorganised' in their patterns? If so, this would suggest that the violence and mutilations were 'ill-conceived' and the direct result of a 'frenzied' attack. In such a case, the labelling of the attacks as 'disorganised' draws attention to aspects not only of the 'style' of the killings but also the 'style of life' of the killer.

This would not be the style of killing attributable to say a 'skilled' worker. The offender who reveals 'confusion' in his attacks is less likely to be a person who deliberately goes in search of potential victims. It is precisely this lack of intelligence applied to the crime that produces the interpretability of the 'patterns' of the offender's actions.

The whole network of aspects of each crime, the many facets it reveals, each can be examined for what it might reveal about the killer. Sadly, prostitutes are very vulnerable people living on the fringes of legality and are at great risk not only from clients but also from other criminals with which they are obliged to mix.

Therefore, the step from being a sexual object to being the subject of violence is not a very big one. One of the clearest facts about an offender's actions is his knowledge and familiarity with a particular area or location. This is a pre-requisite for many violent crimes, particularly serial killings. It is the actual offence itself which forms the focus of all subsequent criminal investigations. Particularly in crimes against people, this will include a very careful consideration of the victims themselves.

In addition, the area in which the crime has been carried out and the type of victim are typically quite consistent for any one offender. Knowledge of the crime area, the nature of the offence, and the route in leaving the crime scene, all point to an offender being resident within reasonable walking distance of the crime scenes. There is a consistency in the actions of criminals who attack people, demonstrated through the viciousness of their actions and the lack of any real awareness of, or feeling for, the consequences of their actions. There will be, in their own lives, social discourse that totally lacks real empathy. The people whose actions take them to the extreme reactions of violent assault and murder are essentially, 'very limited people'.

The 'psychological' examination of crime implies careful attention being paid to many details that might be overlooked in a criminal investigation. It is the careful consideration of *patterns of behaviour* rather than individual 'clues' that is the hallmark of this approach. The distinct characteristics of serial killers are embedded in how, where and when they commit their crimes, but most particularly, where.

It is the consistency of place that allows us to understand and predict the offender's actions. A man does not plan to visit an area of prostitutes in order to kill them secretly based on the reputation of that area alone. He must have had some direct contact with the services available. Did the Ripper have lodgings in the Whitechapel area?

If he did, then this would explain to some extent how he was able to move around freely at night through the maze of back streets and courts. It is a known fact that walking the streets looking for possible targets is common among serial killers. The targets of the Rippers' crimes, the women on the street, and where they were found, tells us something about the offender's psychological characteristics. The locations where his victims were contacted show that the killer was familiar with the ways of street prostitutes. The regularity with which he approaches women in that area of Whitechapel provides a key to his habits.

The 'Ripper' never committed two offences at the same location. This is a pattern often revealed in a 'cautious' offender. No matter how concealed the location of the crime, there is always a risk of returning there. In this change of venue for each of the five murders, the 'Ripper' has demonstrated the extent of his geographical range of activity. Since the 'Ripper' case remains *the* classic serial murder case, offender and psychological profiles can only be applied speculatively. This case has been evaluated by applying these modern techniques. They do not reveal the identity of the offender, but had they been available during the investigation in 1888, then the outcome may well have been very different. Consequently, the Ripper case is never closed and continues to provide a fertile ground for further research as well as speculation.

Chapter Four: An Overview Of The Case

'Jack the Ripper' was the popular name given to a serial killer who murdered a number of prostitutes in the East End of London in 1888. This name originated from a letter written by someone claiming to be the killer, which was received by the media and the police at the time the killings were being committed.

The murders took place within one mile of each other and involved the districts of Whitechapel, Spitalfields and Aldgate, lying within the City of London itself. Jack the Ripper has remained popular for numerous reasons.

He was not the first serial killer in history but probably the first to appear in a large metropolis such as London. It was the media coverage that made the series of murders a 'new' thing, something the world had not experienced before. The press was also partly responsible for creating the many myths surrounding the Ripper.

This ended up turning a serial killer into a 'bogeyman', who has now become one of the most famous, or infamous, figures in criminal history. The residue of the responsibility lies chiefly with the Ripper himself. He may have been a sexual killer, but he was also bent on terrifying a whole city long after he had disappeared from view.

Finally, the Ripper was never caught and brought to justice. It is the mysteries surrounding this killer that both add to the romance of the case, and create an intellectual conundrum that people still strive to solve.

This case has been described as the 'greatest murder sensation of the Victorian era'. The brutality, the serial nature of the killings, and the failure of the police to catch anyone all contribute to making it the biggest story of the day. It remains unclear exactly how many women the

Ripper actually killed, but it is now generally accepted that the total attributed to his hand were the canonical five. However, at the time, the public, the press, and even some elements of the police themselves believed that the killer was responsible for as many as nine murders.

In a time before forensic science and even fingerprinting were established, the only way to prove someone committed a murder was either to catch them in the act or to obtain a confession from the suspect.

Unfortunately, the Whitechapel murders fall into this period of time. One important feature of the case is that not one but two police forces were involved in the investigation of the murders.

The Metropolitan Police, more commonly referred to as 'Scotland Yard', had responsibility for all crimes committed in the Boroughs of London, with the exception of the City itself. The 'square mile' within the heart of the City, had its own police force, the City of London Police, just as it does today.

When Catherine Eddowes, the fourth of the five victims was killed in Mitre Square, this location was in the City Police's territory, and it was this incident that brought them into the Ripper investigations.

It is commonly believed that the 'rank and file' in both respective police forces worked well together. However, there is also evidence that the senior ranks in both forces did not function amicably. Other than attending post-mortem examination and collecting witness statements, there was little else the Metropolitan Police could do at the time.

Given the high-profile nature of the Whitechapel murders, a considerable police effort was mounted to catch the individual. During the course of the whole investigation, it is believed that over 2,000 people were questioned and over 300 suspects actively interviewed by the Metropolitan Police CID before being released. After the first murder of

Mary Ann Nichols on 31 August 1888, the Commissioner, Charles Warren, assigned several officers from Scotland Yard to assist Detective Inspector Edmund Reid, who led the investigation. Encouraged by Warren, a group of local volunteers formed the *Whitechapel Vigilance Committee*, who contributed to the hunt for the killer. This group supplemented police patrols on the streets and even hired private investigators to conduct independent inquiries.

Police investigators were being compounded by the media furore surrounding the murders, with the popular press receiving hundreds of letters regarding the case, including some claiming to be from the killer himself. It was in one of the most prominent of these letters, referred to as the *"Dear Boss"* letter, that the pseudonym Jack the Ripper originated. This and the *"Saucy Jacky"* postcard were given a level of credibility because of the fact that they included information that was not public knowledge at the time they were received.

As a result, Commissioner Warren allowed the publication of the *Dear Boss* letter in the hope that the handwriting was recognisable to someone who may be able to identify its author. Both the letter and postcard were later deemed to be hoaxes, perpetrated by journalists hoping to boost public interest, and obviously, their sales.

A package received by the Secretary of the Whitechapel Vigilance Committee, George Lust, has been traditionally considered to be a more credible communication from the actual killer. This has been referred to as the *From Hell Letter*, which was written in different handwriting to the others. Also, it was not signed 'Jack the Ripper', and it included a portion of a human kidney, allegedly taken from the body of Catherine Eddowes.

After examination by the physician Dr Thomas Openshaw, from Whitechapel London Hospital, it was determined that it was a human left kidney. It did match that taken from Eddowes's body. Unfortunately, little further evidence could be deduced beyond that, and it was not pursued.

    An understrength police force was not the only problem facing the Metropolitan Police during the period of the Whitechapel murders. It appears that disciplinary issues had resulted in 215 officers being arrested for being 'drunk on duty' in 1863. The lack of adequate discipline and general low morale within the force could be seen as a reason for the police's failure to catch the killer after the death of the first victim, Mary Nichols.

    Police inaction could also be seen to have impacted upon the investigation of the second murder, that of Annie Chapman. Witnesses at her inquest gave evidence that they notified a local police constable about the discovery of her body. They were told by that constable to inform someone else about it, because the constable was not allowed to leave his position, due to 'organisational' regulations.

    Preserving the Ripper crime scenes was of vital importance to the ongoing investigation. It can be seen that the 'lapsed' organisational nature of the Metropolitan Police contributed to the ultimate failure in apprehending the killer. Crime scene investigation (CSI) was an unrefined disciple at the time of the murders. However, several command decisions made by Commissioner Warren undoubtedly contributed to the police failure to locate the killer. The most notorious of these actions was his destruction of evidence in the case of the Goulston Street 'graffiti'.

    After the 'double murder' on 30 September, police attempted to trace the movements of the killer, following the murder of Catherine Eddowes in Mitre Square. Given that the 'graffiti' above the evidence taken from the scene (blood-stained apron piece), it was reasonable for police to infer that it had been left as a warning message by the killer. Since the Ripper was suspected of having previously communicated with police and the media with the *Dear Boss* letter and the *Saucy Jacky* postcard, the Goulston Street 'graffiti' could have proven to be highly useful as a verifiable example of his writing style, and could provide clues to his possible background.

Despite objections raised by the City Police, Warren and the local inspector, Thomas Arnold, agreed that the 'graffiti' should be removed as soon as possible. This was in order to prevent a potential riot developing. It is believed that a City Police detective had waited at the scene until it was light to take a photograph of this 'graffiti', but this potentially vital piece of evidence was destroyed before any pictures could be taken.

Warren's decision to remove the 'graffiti' was in direct opposition to the basic tenets of any police investigation – the preservation of evidence. Without a photograph of the message, it was now impossible to compare the handwriting to that of any of the letters supposedly received from the Ripper. This error not surprisingly, caused friction between the attending officers of both forces. Whilst Warren's fear of increasing anti-Semitic tension in the area was undoubtedly valid, the decision to destroy this evidence in an attempt to prevent this frustrated the investigation.

The Whitechapel murders of 1888 proved to be a significant challenge for the Metropolitan Police, and came at a time of significant upheaval which impacted upon their ability to conduct a through and efficient investigation. Due to resignations and re-organisation within the CID, this resulted in a lack of direction and leadership. It is impossible to pinpoint one single issue that led to the police failure to catch the Ripper. There was a wide range of suspects, but also a lack of clarity about what actually constituted a Ripper killing.

It is fair comment to say that the investigation into the murders was hindered by a sense of institutional failure within the Metropolitan Police at the time. These issues were aggravated by an increasingly politicised nature of the police hierarchy, at a time when the threat of political violence and disorder was reaching a crescendo.

The Home Office, in particular, was active in ensuring that the opinion of high ranking officers were in tune with those of the government. Regrettably, the crimes attributed to the Ripper, were not considered to be the most urgent issues for the Metropolitan Police at the time.

The organisation was ravaged by internal conflict, the role of the force, and its relative autonomy from government. It was these issues that distracted the police during a critical investigation. These undoubtedly contributed to their failure to identify the Ripper, and bring a serial killer to justice.

What distinguished the Ripper murders was mutilation – gratuitous damage to the bodies after death. By this diagnostic yardstick, the series of murders began and ended within a two-month period. Yet, in terms of public reactions to them, the killings extended well over a year. At the core of the fear caused by serial murder, was the incomprehensibility of what was actually taking place. The killer's motivation and actions were beyond the experience of daily life and, as such, they were impossible to comprehend.

It was this *unknown* element that was feared the most. The Whitechapel murderer, the brutal killing of at least five women, was very real. The idea that a violent male killer was able to disembowel his victims without being apprehended, has given hundreds of serial killers a *virtual licence* to repeat his crimes ever since 1888. The lack of closure and the failure to catch the killer, have contributed to the creation of a mythology surrounding the

Ripper.

However, it was also the addition of intense media interest in the case which projected the case into a global phenomenon. Public interaction with the murders was almost unprecedented, and this interest has been sustained ever since. In addition to the contradictions and unreliability of contemporary accounts, attempts to identify the killer have also been hampered by a lack of any significant forensic evidence.

From a purely sociological point of view, the Ripper murders and the impoverished lifestyles of his victims drew attention to the poor living conditions in the East End of London during the period of the killings. This served to galvanise public opinion against overcrowding and insanitary slums.

In the two decades following the murders, the worst of these slums were cleared and demolished. However, the streets and some remaining buildings still survive.

The legend of the Ripper is still promoted by various organised guided tours around the murder locations, which attract international visitors annually.

Jack the Ripper features prominently in numerous works of fiction and in those that straddle the boundary between fact and fiction, which deal exclusively with the murders themselves, such as this present work. These, collectively, make it one of the most written-about true crime subjects of all time.

During the 1970s, it was the English author Colin Wilson who coined the term *Ripperology* to describe the study of the case by both professional and amateur contributors. Over the last decade, more evidence has emerged around the Whitechapel murders, and research continues into the mystery of Jack the Ripper than at any other time since the case was officially closed in 1892. I leave the final word to the American author K Lonsdale writing in 2002, who provides a very fitting and apposite conclusion to this work.

"Jack the Ripper remains a definitional paradox. He is both an historical figure, and a discursive presence. He is simultaneously nobody, somebody and everybody."

Selected Bibliography

BEGG, P *Jack the Ripper: The Uncensored Facts: A Documented History of the Whitechapel Murders of 1888*, (London, Robson Books, 1988)

BEGG, P, FIDO, M & SKINNER, K *The Jack the Ripper A to Z*, (London, Headline, 1996)

CAMPS, FE & BARKER, R *The Investigation of Murder*, (London, Michael Joseph, 1966)

CULLEN, T *Autumn of Terror*, (London, The Bodley Head, 2002)

EDDLESTON, J *Jack the Ripper: An Encyclopedia*, (London, Metro Publishing, 2002)

EGAN-WHITTINGTON, R *Jack the Ripper: The Definitive Casebook*, (Amberley Publishing, Stroud, Gloucestershire, 2018)

EVANS, SP & SKINNER, K *The Ultimate Jack the Ripper Sourcebook: An Illustrated Encyclopedia*, (London, Robinson, 2000)

FARSON, D *Jack the Ripper*, (London, Michael Joseph, 1972)

FELDMAN, PH *Jack the Ripper: The Final Chapter*, (London, Virgin Books, 1997)

FIDO, M *The Crimes, Detection and Death of Jack the Ripper*, (London, Weidenfeld & Nicholson, 1987)

FISHER, JC *Killer Among Us: Public Reactions to Serial Murder*, (Westport, Conn: Praeger, 1997)

HARRIS, M *The Ripper File*, (London, WH Allen, 1989)

HARRISON, P *Jack the Ripper: The Mystery Solved*, (London, Robert Hale, 1991)

KNIGHT, S *Jack the Ripper: The Final Solution*, (London, Harrap, 1994)

LONSDALE, K "Rounding Up The Usual Suspects: Echoing Jack the Ripper" in *Functions of Victorian Culture at the Present Time*, (Ohio University Press, 2002)

McCORMICK, D *The Identity of Jack the Ripper*, (London, Jarrold, 1959)

ODELL, R *Jack the Ripper in Fact and Fiction*, (London, Harrap, 1965)

PALEY, B *Jack the Ripper: The Simple Truth* (London, Headline, 1995)

RUMBELOW, D *The Complete Jack the Ripper*, (London. W.H.Allen, 1987)

SUGDEN, P *The Complete History of Jack the Ripper*, (London, Robinson, 1994)

WILSON, C & ODELL, R *Jack the Ripper: Summing Up and Verdict*, (London, Bantam Press, 1987)

WOLF, AP *Jack the Myth: A New Look at the Ripper*, (London, Robert Hale, 1993)

Printed in Great Britain
by Amazon